EDUCATIONAL TOURISM

By

Marsh P Lee

DISCOVERY PUBLISHING HOUSE PVT. LTD.

NEW DELHI-110 002

First Published - 2011

Reprinted - 2016

ISBN: 978-81-8356-943-9

Educational Tourism

Published by:

DISCOVERY PUBLISHING HOUSE PVT. LTD.

4383/4B, Ansari Road, Darya Ganj

New Delhi-110 002 (India)

Phone: +91-11-23279245, 43596064-65

Fax: +91-11-23253475

E-mail: discoverypublishinghouse@gmail.com

sales@discoverypublishinggroup.com

web: www.discoverypublishinggroup.com

Printed at:

Infinity Imaging Systems

Delhi

PREFACE

The educational tourism phenomenon that is attaining universal popularity and jumping on the bandwagon, people from far-flung corners of the world are especially considering India as an important destination for their educational tours. These tours are especially focused on having a share of the educational experiences available in the country and also to enhance knowledge on the rich Indian history and culture.

The various aspects of educational tourism include an educational program in which the participants chose to travel to a region or country in specific groups with the aim of learning something from the visited region. In specific terms, educational tourism is all about visiting and then staying in a foreign country for more than 24 hours and not more than one year in a row for the purpose of availing short term language classes, education in school / universities, vocational and other specialized courses.

Going abroad for higher education is not a new phenomenon in our country.Educational tourism is one of the fastest growing areas of the travel and tourism and one that is too often overlooked by tourism professionals and marketers. For example, many meetings and conventions have either an educational component to them or serve their members by being educational instruments. Often educational tourism is called by other names, such as career enhancement, job development or self-actualization experiences.

Educational tourism then comes in a wide variety of formats, yet despite the differences all forms of educational tourism have a number of points in common. Among these are, the idea that travel is as much about self-improvement as it is about relaxation, that learning can be fun, and that learning is for people of all ages. This book is informative and interesting one for all those students who are planning to study abroad and see tourists spots too.

—Author

CONTENTS

CHAPTER–1

INTRODUCTION TO EDUCATIONAL TOURISM

The concept of educational tourism is not a new phenomenon. From remote times, students and professors have travelled to foreign lands to improve their intellectual knowledge and/or increase their professional prestige; travelling has always permitted the acquisition of new tools for professional practice as well as contact with other cultures which favors an integral education.

Nowadays, this phenomenon has acquired very significant magnitudes, with an increasing number of foreign students choosing Argentina for their studies. Determining factors are the diversity of college, university and master courses, as well as the international acknowledgment of the excellence of our academic institutions and the educational quality of the Spanish language teaching centers.

Another relevant component is the trend to choose exotic countries; Argentina being one of such because of the multiplicity of landscapes and cultural environments in which the students interact with the natural, social and cultural world.

Educational tourism is one of the fastest growing areas of the travel and tourism and one that is too often overlooked by tourism professionals and marketers. For example, many meetings and conventions have either an educational component to them or serve their members by being educational instruments. Often educational tourism is called by other names, such as career development, job opportunities or self-actualization experiences.

Japan is world famous for high quality technical education with abundance of nature beauty. Japan is also known for its strong educational system which offers broad range of educational scopes here. The striking fact associated with the ever-increasing popularity of educational tourism in Japan is that short term courses are available in Japanese universities and other educational institutions at a very affordablel fee compared to other universities and this is hugely attracting foreigners to partake in the Japanese educational system.. Foreigners are hugely attracted by the cost-effectiveness of these courses and as these courses throw light on different aspects of Japanese culture and history, the tourists studying them are introduced to the variegated facets of Japanese cultural experience in an effective manner.

FORMS OF EDUCATION

Tourism was used at key points in British history to educate people. It is possible to argue that it was filling an educational role most of the time, at least in its early stages. Virtually all forms of tourism began for educational reasons. Most currently available work underplays this fact, with the possible exception of discussions on the Grand Tour. Holloway makes a statement about "tourists and locals alike widening their horizons" almost as an afterthought to a short discussion of socio-cultural problems. Cooper et al refer to myths surrounding tourism which "should be broken", pointing out "Tourism is not purely for the purposes of leisure. It also includes business tourism, pilgrimages and tourism for health purposes".

A later chapter on "The Future of Tourism" makes only passing mention to `new' tourists looking for "rewarding activities to fill their leisure time and to satisfy their cultural, intellectual and sporting interests", but it is only in the context of the needs of certain market segments in "multi-interest travel". Voase (1995) in an interesting and useful book touches on many aspects of tourism which relate to education, without dealing with it as a perspective. A chapter about the future discusses economics, global warming, people in tourism, sustainability, transport and fashions, but not tourism as an educative activity.

Ryan's "The Chase of a Dream, the End of a Play" (in Ryan, 1997, p23) refers to tourism as an educative process within the context of sociological discussion. The historical references consider tourism largely as leisure and escapism. Hollinshead's "Heritage Tourism Under Post-modernity: Truth and the Past" in the same collection as Ryan (1997), shows how great a gap there is between the sociological critic on the one hand and the teacher of history on the other, as the scholarship of Samuel's "Theatres of Memory" (1994) illustrates. Hollinshead paints a pessimistic picture of a world in which all history teaching outside the classroom or library appears impossible since it long ago succumbed to a conspiracy by various forces of darkness. There is little illumination in this kind of writing for the history teacher working out of the classroom. History teachers know well that all interpretations - including books and academic papers - of the world take particular viewpoints, selecting, interpreting and presenting reality as they see it. Even so, a re-assessment of tourism which hopes to be accepted at a higher academic level will have to establish a credible, theoretical and practical counter-argument to the Hollinshead kind of view.

Weiler and Hall edited a collection of papers in "Special Interest Tourism" (1992) which look at a number of case studies and review some sectors. They point to the "diversity of market segments and products ... encompassed within the rubric of `special interest tourism'" and "the limited amount of research that has been done" (p199). The book unfortunately suffers from being more a collection of snapshots of relevant areas, but the opening chapter does attempt an overview. Sadly, it remains only a collection of separate perspectives such as marketing, ethics and green tourism, rather than shining a well-focused new light on the whole issue.

Within the book, the paper on "Educational Travel" is particularly disappointing in its attempt to take a historical perspective. It makes only two references, the first to the Grand Tour as the originator of educational travel and second to 'Chautauqua'. "The modem-day learning vacation concept seems to have originated at Chautauqua, a residential institution in New York. Initiated in 1874 by a Methodist minister and an Ohio businessman, Chautauqua blends the concept of an outdoor recreation setting with social activities and learning opportunities". This American example is interesting and important as it led to some 12,000 similar centres within the United States, but they were largely centres where general educational activities took place, rather than centres where people discovered their (temporary) new environments through first-hand contact. As a perspective on educational tourism it is disappointing. Another look must be taken at the history of tourism forms.

The pilgrimage was an early form of informal education as it brought devotees closer to knowledge of sacred sites and introduced them to new experiences and knowledge, but not in any didactic way. Prehistoric pilgrimages took place to centres associated with magical properties and religious beliefs, and specifically Christian pilgrimages were undertaken at least from the late fourth century AD. Around 610 AD pilgrims could buy a guide to the churches of Rome - an early aid to visitor interpretation .

The Canterbury Pilgrims, following a well-used route from Winchester or London to Canterbury Cathedral relied on a growing infrastructure of tracks, inns and stables in order to make their journey. In Poland, the monastery of Jasna Gora in Czestochowa, founded in 1382, received thousands of pilgrims each year to see an image of the Blessed Virgin Mary housed there: by 1682 it was around 140,000, and by the present day it sometimes welcomes a million in a single year. Historically, each visit was part of a process of communication and teaching in which what the pilgrims had seen and experienced was fed back to others in their own villages and towns .

The nature of the Grand Tour as an education for the sons of the English gentry has been well covered. Rooted in the explorations of Queen Elizabeth I's age, the Grand Tour was encouraged by her as a means of training men for government. Feifer (1985, p64) quotes James Howell's "Instructions for Forraine Travel" (1642) comparing the stay-at-home with the traveller. "To run over and traverse the world by hearsay ... other men's eyes ... is but a confused and imperfect kind of speculation, which leaveth but weak and distrustful notions" said Howell of the former, and praised the first-hand view of the latter: "the eye ... as through a clear and crystal casement we ... in one instant comprehend half the whole universe".

Though the later Grand Tourists were more interested in pleasure than in being educated, the whole experience remained educational in the widest of senses. Even time spent in a brothel would teach the young buck about life. The part played by Grand Touring in British culture is well documented, but there was an important influence on industry and technology, too see Armytage, 1961 p 96 on the influence of the Canal du Midi on the British Industrial Revolution, and Klingender, 1972, pp 85-86 on de Loutherbourg and dramatic presentation.

Thomas Cook's entry into the history of travelling was made by a desire to educate. The 1841 railway excursion from Leicester to Loughborough took five hundred people to an open space where Cook, a Baptist preacher, could educate them about the evils that he saw in alcohol. However successful he might have been in his chosen aim, he was certainly successful in his method. With a combination of the excitement of open-wagon rail travel, the leisurely nature of the day, and the ambience of a different environment, the Leicester folk must have been in a receptive and tolerant mood. No consumer motivator could ask for more. Thomas Cook's contributions were all about packaging travel, an attention to detail, and the providing of quality experiences, but above all the enjoyment by his customers of discovering new places.

The growth of seaside holidays is also well documented. From them it can be seen that even the hedonism of the seaside existed alongside the wonders of discovery. In 1788 Catherine Hutton from Birmingham wrote home about the people she encountered in Blackpool: "The Boltoners are sincere, good humoured and noisy. The Manchestrians reserved and purse-proud, the Liverpoolians free and open as the ocean upon which they get their riches."

And while Blackpool was a place of social encounter, it was also one with an Opera House, an Aquarium, a Menagerie, a Winter Gardens with "high class concerts", and its famous Circus. From 1910 even the Pleasure Beach had its "edutainment" in devices like the Naval Spectatorium which used 360-degree film projection and mechanical devices to present representations of the American Civil War, and later, World War I naval battles (Turner and Palmer, 1976). Such devices were the norm for resorts which wanted to entertain their visitors, and indeed, Scarborough retains its "Naval Warfare" event to this day.

Presenting the wonders of the world has been a foundation for entertainment ever since the earliest bards told their stories. In due course the resorts of the industrialised world built fair grounds, theatres, museums, galleries, menageries and gardens drawing upon the culture, artefacts, flora and fauna of the world around them. Fairs like the Kursaal at Southend-on-Sea, Dreamland at Margate, and the Paradium at Great Yarmouth (Pearson, 1991) derived excitement from representations, however distorted, of reality. The huge Coney Island parks in New York almost became international expositions in their own right by building theatres, cinemas and other shows (Snow and Wright, 1976). They were in direct line of descent from the London, Paris, Vienna and Chicago Exhibitions long before Disney.

Visiting great houses and museums, and the educational value that related to such excursions, has been a recent subject of analysis. Ousby says that "Travel was a leading instrument of that post-Reformation spirit of enquiry which valued empirical knowledge over abstract speculation or book-learning derived merely from tradition" .

It was during the middle years of the nineteenth century, and in parallel with the beginnings of formalised education for various age groups from young to old, that the practice was established of townspeople and city dwellers making day visits to the country. These were not only for what we might term `escapist' entertainment, but for `self-improvement'.

Local newspapers of the time are full of the accounts of annual outings by social groups from chapels or work-places. There are detailed accounts preserved of the organisation required for the bigger trips, such as the well-known railway excursions from the Bass Breweries. These show how guide books and visits of an `improving nature' were made integral to the excursions by those who organised them. One quotation from the 40-page booklet distributed to 8,000 participants in the 1914 visit to Scarborough will give a flavour:

"The improvements made since our last visit in 1910 consist of deepening the old or West Harbour by about three to four feet, so as to accommodate and give more room for fishing craft of a larger size and to the increasing number of Steam Drifters now engaged in the Herring Fishery, in addition to the Sailing Herring Fishers. The West Pier, where the fish is landed, sold and packed, has been widened - 70 feet being added - and now provides excellent curing and packing spaces for the herring curers and exporters."

A videotaped account given by a retired worker from John Crossley and Sons' carpet mills in Halifax shows in anecdote some of the cultural effects. Mrs Florence Waite took part in a long railway excursion over 30 hours to Edinburgh, Glasgow and the Isle of Bute in 1934 with Crossley's Social Club. The impact made by Edinburgh's particular historic character, and the Clyde's glorious scenery, are clear even after sixty years .Delgado has shown how important the annual excursion was as an escape from the industrial city. In 1912, the Duchess of Sunderland foresaw "A day that is a glimpse of Paradise to the poor little mites who live in the darkness of squalid back courts and the mean streets of our cities", when raising money for a charity sending children on a countryside excursion

Thomas Cook had religious motives (it was his son John Mason Cook who went fully commercial in tourism), believing that through his tours "man has been brought nearer to man and nearer to his Creator" (Brendon, 1991). It must be stressed that Cook began as an evangelist, a communicator, and not a tour operator. However unconsciously, he succeeded because he removed his audience from the stress of everyday life, induced within them a receptive and relaxed frame of mind, and then tried to persuade them to adopt a new lifestyle based on Christianity and, in particular, teetotalism. This aligns with Turner's analysis of the pilgrimage with its ideas of separation, liminality and communitas .

But it also aligns with the principles of propaganda and persuasion of the use of group psychology, removing his audience to a different setting, creating a receptive mood and using crowd psychology to persuade individuals to adopt new attitudes (Brown, 1963 and Jowett and O'Donnell, 1992). Cook's Loughborough excursion operated in terms of communication between people, and between people and environments, depending on the contrasts between Leicester (a city full of the stresses of everyday life), the thrills of the railway journey (excitement, empowerment, and innovation) and the Loughborough destination (comparative arcadia, relaxation, and enjoyment). Cook's aim was to educate, and educate effectively.

A similar set of motives inspired the Reverend T A Leonard. The Congregational minister preached a sermon at Dockray Street Church in Colne in August 1891 in which he criticised the habit some people had of 'laking' about - playing - saying that "the devil wields no small influence over holiday times". Holidays should be taken sensibly, sacredly indeed. Leonard's view was "Speak to the earth and it will teach thee" (Speake, 1993). The idea of education within holidays was present when Leonard went on to encourage a group of thirty men to organise a holiday in Ambleside in 1891, and Caernarfon the next.

By 1893 he was Secretary "of a scheme which embodies a new idea of summer holidays", inviting adult education classes and Pleasant Sunday Associations to join in visits to Ambleside and Keswick, walking by day and enjoying music and `lecturettes' in the evenings. The rambles were conducted by a University companion guide appointed by the National Home Reading Union (Speake, 1993). This was the beginning of the Co-operative Holidays Association, now the Countrywide Holidays Association and operating many holiday homes for its members.

Formal education out of doors is little covered in tourism books, yet it is one which by its variety and early encounter by students must underlie so much of their subsequent interest in travel. A very early example of this activity is that of the herbarizing organised by the Society of Apothecaries of London. This was the practical means by which apprentice apothecaries could be taught to recognise plants which would have medicinal values.

The first one known took place in May of 1620, beginning at 5.00am with a rendezvous at St Paul's in the City. The day was spent out in the country, then relatively close by. Within a short while six excursions a year were being held. After a while a paid official known as the Demonstrator of Plants was employed to lead the excursions, and in 1673 the Chelsea Physic Garden was established as a permanent demonstration area. It has since become an important tourist attraction in its own right. Herbarizings continued up to 1824 when it was decided London was too big to allow for day excursions to open countryside, and the educational practice was abandoned. By then, many botanists had received their introduction to the subject through these events (Allen, 1976).

In 1732 The Society of Dilettante was formed from a group of men who had been on the Grand Tour. The Society helped to pioneer archaeological field study. Geology field teaching was in turn developed from 1804 by Robert Jameson of Edinburgh who took formal field classes as far away as the Western Isles. Geography field teaching in the UK got off to a relatively late start and in 1938 a survey of London schools showed that "hardly a half are able to conduct outdoor field work" (Dilke, 1965 p17). This was despite John Ruskin having said that "the country will become an outer and uncovered classroom, a Divine museum utilised by our teachers" (Reynolds, 1901). Excursions were the exception, rather than the rule.

One did occur in 1886, when Scott Keltie reported to the Royal Geographical society that the children of Gordon's Hospital School, Aberdeen, were "taken out into the country and in a simple, rough but effective, and to them, interesting and instructive way, are taught to draw maps of a small area for themselves" (Dilke, 1965). On the other hand, adult geographers made group excursions quite early. The Manchester Geographical Society went to inspect the new docks in Preston in the autumn of 1887 (Brown, 1971) for example. It should be remembered that individual adult travellers were being drawn towards industrial locations to see the changed landscapes presented from at least the 1780s onwards, as has been seen above. Field Societies, Scientific and Literary Societies and Geographical Societies continued through the nineteenth and twentieth centuries to make such excursions.

The practice widened out in the twentieth as manufacturers like Cadburys and Wedgwoods, anxious to promote their methods and products, opened their doors to all kinds of groups. Lever Brothers joined with the LMS railway company to promote tourism to their factory in Port Sunlight in 1926 (Cole and Durack, 1992). In the 1950s and 1960s both companies handled thousands of adult and school visitors. The present author recalls making visits to factories such as Lotus Shoes in Stone, British Rail Engineering in Crewe, a Co-op Dairy in Llangadog, the Velindre Tinplate Works and the Steel Company of Wales, Port Talbot. The steel and engineering companies used visits for general public relations purposes, the consumer goods makers used them to sell their wares. Even tiny manufacturers got involved, for example Joseph Dobson and Sons of Elland who from 1980 welcomed visitors in order to raise their profiles against their big competitors.

Indeed, Marling has recently shown how even that great icon of theme park tourism, Walt Disney, began with ideas for a "kiddies park" (Marling, 1997). Disney's new Burbank studio of 1939 was laid out on production-line principles. Having seen Snow White, people were asking to see how the animation was done. Disney thought that those who did visit found the whole process boring, and in any case there was none of the fairy tale magic on the production floor. So he began to plan a special area which would show both magic and motion picture production.

Early in the twentieth century it took people like James Fairgrieve, training geography teachers in the 1920s, to foster an interest in school excursions and holidays. He suggested children in east London could begin by finding out "information about the commodities that their fathers are handling". They could look at the doors of Fleet Street to see listed the newspapers of the British Empire as a starting point for discussing its geography. They would continue by making excursions to other places. "This is a benefit not only to the understanding of other lands but to the understanding of the homeland also. In a very real sense the homeland is measured by other lands: also, unless it is seen in its world setting, it is not really understood" (Fairgrieve, 1926). Factory visits were being added by progressive teachers at least from the late 1940s.

The nineteenth century was the great age of self-improving societies, often growing out of church or chapel groups who began to investigate interesting subjects. Others were specifically for self-help. The earliest - and still thriving with its private museum and lecture programme and visits - was the Spalding Gentlemen's' Society, founded in 1710. There were Mechanic's Institutes and worker's educational groups, and the subject societies for literary and scientific pursuits, from botany to geology and geography, many of which organised and ran their own excursions. In the United States similar self-help groups emerged in the diverse and often isolated settlements further west, while in the east urban groups sprang up, and the Chautauqua, already mentioned, had an important effect.

The original Chautauqua started as a summer vacation and training centre for Sunday School teachers at Chautauqua Lake, near to Lake Erie, in New York State. It developed as a place for discussion and debate on classical and current topics. Scholars, actors, speakers and exhibits were arranged, plays put on, great speeches re-made and debates staged (Colorado Chautauqua Association, 1997). Home-reading circles became part of the system, and for a time participants could study for a degree at a Chautauqua University.

The idea was imported to Britain largely through the work of J B Paton, who had been involved in setting up a University Extension in Nottingham. In 1887 Paton formed a small committee with John Percival, Headmaster of Rugby School, and from 1888 they organised Summer Meetings at Oxford with educational courses (Kelly, 1970). This line continued as the growth in the UK of adult education.

By the late nineteenth century the ideas of Frederic Le Play (Beaver, 1962) and then Patrick Geddes (Meller, 1990) had formed the basis for sociological field work with a strong geographical basis. Geddes' ideas has particularly interesting features in the context of the present paper. In Paris in 1878 he visited the International Exhibition and was enthusiastically inspired by the display of the reconstruction of Paris after the Franco-Prussian war of 1870. Returning to Edinburgh he became immersed in ideas of planning and improvement, one step in which was the purchase by him of the old Observatory at the lower end of the Castle Esplanade. It housed (and still does) a camera obscura which was used to project views of the city onto a white `projection table' for visitors to study.

Renamed the Outlook Tower and using whatever small funds and voluntary help that he could muster, Geddes began to create a kind of regional museum. He was also involved in teaching at the Edinburgh Summer Meetings or schools, linking the educational work with the displays in his Outlook Tower and excursions into Edinburgh to encourage city renewal.

Helen Meller, in Patrick Geddes: "Social Evolutionist and City Planner", shows how he absorbed ideas from the efforts of museums to collect and classify social knowledge (Meller, 1990). The Musee Sociale in Paris built on ideas which had been shown at the Paris Exhibitions of 1867, 1878 and 1889 about the study of people and their environs. The International Bibliographical Institute in Brussels was systematically collecting and classifying human knowledge in order to act as a centre of study. Geddes devised an idea for an `Index Museum' in his Outlook Tower with a kind of three-dimensional encyclopaedia of the world installed in it.

Geddes again went to an Exhibition in Paris, this time in 1900, organising a huge programme of lectures and tours in a Summer School there. "Eight hundred classes were held in just 120 days, and the average attendance at these was between 40 and 502" (Meller, 1990). And there at the Exhibition were pavilions and buildings from around the world. Geddes wanted to save them as a permanent `Index Museum', a centre of study of the world's cultures and societies. It failed to happen for reasons of cost and ownership.

Within the Paris Exhibition of 1900 the strands of education (Summer School), tourist attraction (the displays) and inspiration for progress (the ideas communicated by the displays and the School) came together. It did not become permanent: that would happen in museums and inter-activity centres in another age, perhaps more related to heritage than to visions of the future as Geddes wanted, but the principles, firmly based in educative forms of tourism, were all there.

A different - though related - reason was behind the origins of the Scout and Guide movement, which turned mere country visiting into an organised, structured, educationally-motivated activity. "Our business is not merely to keep up smart `show' troops, but to pass as many boys through our character factory as we possibly can: at the same time, the longer the grind that we can give them the better men they will be in the end" (Baden-Powell, 1908). Scouting was one of the occupations which, along with inspirational books like "Bevis: The Story of A Boy" (Jefferies, 1882) and "Swallows and Amazons" (Ransome, 1929) created the idea of adventure holidays which is at the heart of modem children's activity tourism. Jefferies educated his readers about the countryside: Baden-Powell trained his, through "Scouting For Boys" into adventurers who grew inwardly through their interaction with the rural environment.

As Michael Rosenthal shows, much of scout culture drew upon the works of the Anglo-American author, Ernest Thompson Seaton (Rosenthal, 1986). Between the 1880s and the 1900s Seton spread ideas of what he called Woodcraft' as a way for young American males to learn from, and be entertained by, life in the great outdoors. He based his philosophy on the native North American culture and outlined a national movement based on features from his reading of native life, with a liberal dash of European chivalric ideas thrown in. Baden-Powell's movement adopted some of the ideas, but Seton's Woodcraft Indians continue still as a separate organisation. There was also an influence on the European Woodcraft Folk movement which grew amongst people who wanted a youth organisation which avoided what they saw as Baden-Powell's establishmentism and military leanings. Within one sector of tourism therefore it is possible to follow the development of a clear political/philosophical strand.

During the nineteenth century the growth and diversity of schooling allowed experimentation in terms of organisation and curriculum. Influenced by Rousseau's ideas about the importance of an individual's development some innovations were made which tried to relate teaching environments to the pupil's needs. In England, Cecil Reddie founded Abbotsholme School in 1889 as somewhere which could take a boy "to train him how to live" (Lawson and Silver, 1973). This meant daily, outdoor activities such as drill, sports, river bathing, running, carpentry and gardening.

Just after World War I Kurt Hahn co-founded Salem School in Germany with Prince Max von Baden, in which the development of character and selfdiscipline were foremost. Abbotsholme had had an influence. With the arrival of Nazism Kurt Hahn was forced to leave, and he moved to Britain_ In late 1933 he opened Gordonstoun School in Scotland, with a disciplinarian programme which included ideas of service to the nearby community. From 1935 onwards boys were enrolled as HM Coastguards, and they later operated a small fire brigade. The `Moray Badge' scheme was devised with tests in athletics, expeditions, and life-saving, partly in response to a national debate about the poor quality of fitness in young people (Hahn, 1957). It is interesting to note the similarities to matching fears expressed at the turn of the century about the health and character of boys which helped lead to the Boy Scouts.

Out of the Badge scheme came three experimental; residential summer schools in Invemess-shire and Morayshire. Their success led in turn to the formation of the Outward Bound schools, this time in Wales, at Aberdovey, to which Gordonstoun had been evacuated on the outbreak of war. From 1941 an Outward Bound Sea School commenced operation, offering courses to young men from industry, not only in maritime activities, but also 30-mile mountain country expeditions (Hahn, 1957). The Outward Bound movement has also grown and expanded its activities to a number of British and European centres.

In Germany the idea of the school excursion had gained ground rapidly from 1907 and the formation of the 'wandervogel' at Jena in January that year. Its aims were "to promote rambles and excursions of German boys in their own and other neighbourhoods, and thus to awaken in them a taste for the beauties of nature, and to give them opportunities of learning to know their German homeland and its people at first hand" (Thomson and Haehnel, 1909). Local associations were set up and older children encouraged to qualify as guides. Books and maps were bought and could be hired out to non-members. Travel and overnight accommodation were to be simple - fourth-class rail and country barns.

Earlier still, the Eberfeld 'Realgymnasium' was one of several schools which held indoor lessons until noon and then gymnastics or excursions. On six afternoons in the summer term the whole four hundred children at Eberfeld would march out of town behind a band, the older children going the furthest, and teachers instructing the pupils along the way. Games would round off the excursion, for which six hours was allowed. The government extended the Whit holiday to allow higher classes make longer journeys to places like the Westerwald, Taunus and Eiffel districts. Up to twenty boys and their masters might make a fortnight's visit to somewhere like Italy. The days started early and consisted of long walks followed by evening recreation ("beer and songs") and summaries by the boys of what they had done - often given in foreign languages. The pupils paid themselves in advance, with poorer boys charged less, but "for poor masters no funds were provided" (Bahre, 1901). It is noteworthy that German interest in exploring environments seems to have underpinned the country's ideas in gestalt psychology, to which reference will be made later.

Another organisation began in Germany in the same year, 1907, that Baden-Powell was holding his first scout camp on Brownsea Island in Poole Harbour. A teacher, Richard Schirmann, opened his school to a group of children from slum areas, so that they could enjoy a countryside holiday. Two years later Altena Town Council and a local businessman gave money to turn Burg Altena into a hostel.

It was the start of the 'wandervogel' movement, anti-militarist, anti-machinery, pro-country life. Britain set up its first hostel in 1930 though a water-supply problem forced it to close soon afterwards. The YHA dates from that year, and the next year saw no fewer than twenty hostels open (Coburn, 1950). Country life, exploration and adventure were the aims of all their visitors.

In Britain all of these strands became woven together after 1945 and new ones were added. The Field Studies Council in Britain opened its first centre in Suffolk in 1946, and the first local authority centre, White Hall near Buxton, opened in 1950 (Parker and Meldrum, 1973). National Parks, open air museums, commercially-run adventure centres, stately homes and historic houses, castles and wartime defences, zoos and sea-life centres, gardens and country parks, heritage centres and inter-active science centres, factory tours and craft demonstration units made their appearances on ever larger scales. Were these just part of a heritage industry making new money, or an extension of the very long growth of educational tourism? School visits, especially when linked to the National Curriculum, can provide the bread-and-butter visitor income that they need to survive.

This account of some of the educational aspects of tourism is not complete, nor could it be within the confines of a discussion paper. Nor does it attempt to discuss in detail who benefited from each, nor just how much benefit there was, nor how prejudiced or enlightened any of it might have been. What is important here is the acknowledgement of the frequent close liaison that there has always been in tourism with education. It is fair, and appropriate, to say that all forms of information and opinion, whether expressed between individuals, through the mass media, or in education, are subject to limitations on access, quality and objectivity. The point is that tourism is just as good, or just as bad, as they are. But it has, like them, a potential for being beneficial.

The educational tourism sector is also spreading its wings in the Malaysia due to the use of highly standardized English in various educational institutions across the country, cost-effectiveness of courses available here and a higher degree of academic standards. Moreover, a range of study tours and student exchange programs are also facilitated by Indian universities welcoming students from different parts of the world, this too has led to a tremendous growth in the educational tourism industry..

Taking important lessons within the confines of a classroom is the first and foremost way of augmenting knowledge and it is altogether certain that knowledge can be gained by reading books, talking to people and also by opting for other means of communication.

This is exactly the educational tourism phenomenon that is attaining universal popularity and jumping on the bandwagon, people from far-flung corners of the world are especially considering India as an important destination for their educational tours. These tours are especially focused on having a share of the educational experiences available in the country and also to enhance knowledge on the rich Indian history and culture.

The various aspects of educational tourism include an educational program in which the participants chose to travel to a region or country in specific groups with the aim of learning something from the visited region. In specific terms, educational tourism is all about visiting and then staying in a foreign country for more than 24 hours and not more than one year in a row for the purpose of availing short term language classes, education in school / universities, vocational and other specialized courses.

Most importantly, comprehensive educational tourism packages are offered by the Indian universities which are prepared in a way that it is possible for the tourist to gain a firm hold on the specific subject matter. Further, as the people visiting India in search of wholesome learning experience gain ample scope to educate themselves on the history and culture of the country, wildlife and ecology, flora and fauna of the nation in addition to gaining expertise in their own course material, the number of visitors looking for educational opportunities in India has increased tremendously making India the nerve center of global educational tourism.

For many in the world of education, the months of May and June represent the end of the academic year and the start of tourism's high season. Thus, from the perspective of the tourism industry as the academic year wanes, new tourism educational opportunities begin to wax.

Educational tourism then comes in a wide variety of formats, yet despite the differences all forms of educational tourism have a number of points in common. Among these are, the idea that travel is as much about self-improvement as it is about relaxation, that learning can be fun, and that learning is for people of all ages. However, in the present times, apart from these popular methods of acquiring knowledge, travelling to foreign locations and enrolling in short term courses in those countries is getting popular as an effective method of gaining knowledge in a specific subject/field. What is interesting is that while visiting a foreign country on an educational trip, the visitor also gets to know the culture and history of its people, the titbits on people's lifestyle and architecture.

Here are just some of the opportunities for your location to attract educational tourism income.

EDUCATIONAL TOURISM OPPORTUNITIES

School Trips

It may pay your community to create reasons for school children to visit. While these trips rarely translate directly into overnight stays, they can help promote your tourism product in two ways: (1) children may bring their parents back for a longer visit and (2) they aid the local restaurant business.

Alternative 'Spring Break' Travel Experiences

This form of educational travel may be the most controversial form, so much so that some may argue that Spring Break travel has nothing to do with education. This form of travel only works if you have geography that lends itself, be it snow covered mountains or beaches with palm trees. In either case consider the pros and cons of Spring Break tourism. Often Spring breakers add extra tourism costs in the form or police and sanitation overtime.

Study Abroad Experiences

Most major universities around the world promote some form of foreign travel for their students. Study abroad experiences provide students with anything from 6-week intensive study sessions to a full year of cultural and linguistic immersion. US universities that have long seen themselves as student-exporters have now come to realize that non-English speaking students seek US study abroad adventures too. Students often travel not only within their destination country of choice but throughout that county and even to neighboring lands. The goal here is to widen the educational experience so that university students do not only know their own culture but also that of at least one other nation.

Seminar Vacations and Senior Seminars

These types of travel experience especially appeal to those who have recently retired. Programs such as elder hostel provide senior citizens with everything from a chance to learn about the arts to physics lectures or astronomy. They are conducted at camps and on campuses around the world.

Closely related to seminar vacations are 'hands-on enhanced experience' vacations. For example, each year thousands of people travel to Israel to learn something about an archeological dig and then pay to participate on such a dig.

Skill Enhancement Vacations

These are trips that range from learning how to build houses to how to protect the ecology. Nations such as Costa Rica have been extremely successful with eco-tourism in which they combine lessons on how to protect the world's ecology with the travel experience.

Educational Cruises

These cruises combine all of the fun of a cruise with lectures on specific subjects. Educational cruises have the advantage that people who take them tend to have common interest and therefore have a greater possibility of making new friends while acquiring new knowledge.

EDUCATIONAL TOURISM TIPS

Educational tourism offers another major advantage. It does not need to be weather dependent, a community does not need special geography and usually most of the needed infrastructure is already in place. Choose your preferred field of study at uop to give you the advantage you need in life. In order to take advantage of these educational tourism products consider the following:

Develop Tourism Educational Inventory

Work with local schools and universities to know what is of educational interest to visitors. While historical sites are an important part of educational tourism, do not neglect other aspects. For example, can you incorporate a local science lab into your list of educational offerings? Is there a way to work with a local school in order to teach an athletic skill?

For example, Portugal's Pierre de Coubertin Soccer Academy, located just outside of Oporto will teach individual how to incorporate the art of soccer into a person's business life. While there adult students can learn soccer, get in shape, sample Portuguese wine, and visit Portugal's grape and wine country. These skill enhancement trips are a great way for working people to de-stress while learning a new skill or perfecting an older one.

Find Locals to Teach Others

Find local people who would be willing to teach others a skill or impart some form of knowledge. These people become local attractions and the tourism industry can help them to earn extra money at the same time.

Reach Conference Planners

Make sure that conference planners know that you can offer local educational experiences as a way to enhance their conference. Offer local experiences to conferences and seminars that add both professional knowledge and personal growth. Indicate that you are willing to include family members who may also be attending the conference.

Treat the People Appropriately

Be careful of who works in educational tourism. Often tour guides and other educational tourism staff members forget that educational tourism is based around people on vacation. These people do not want to be treated as children. Never forget that they are paying guests.

Establish Regional Tourism Study Groups

One of the best ways to promote educational tourism is to be involved in it yourself. Pick a topic for the year and help hotels and other tourism establishments know that visitors are welcome to come for one or more sessions.

Educational tourism then comes in a great variety of formats; places seeking to enhance their educational tourism product however have to first consider who their market is and what they have to teach others that is special or unique. Educational tourism is a way to use better our facilities, especially during off seasons, and increase interpersonal understanding through unique and creative travel experiences.

Educational Tourism in ThailandImagine studying in a country like Thailand... Imagine rewarding yourself with a weekend on the beach after a hard week's study, or trekking through the jungle as soon as your exams are over! Whether for full blown degree programs or short vocational courses, more and more people are making Thailand part of their educational objectives and becoming 'Educational Tourists'.

With fewer Thai students studying abroad over the last decade, foreign universities opened campuses in Thailand or made agreements with Thai universities to run 'Dual' (or 'Twinning') degree programs - foreign degrees run at Thai universities. As a result, Thailand has a huge choice of international-level education options and is a major draw for students all over the world looking for world-class education.

Of course, to benefit from higher education at an 'English-medium' university, students must understand English well. For many years there has been a booming domestic market for English language courses in Thailand; a market driven by Thai students who appreciate the benefits of studying with a native English speaking teacher. As a result, there are countless teaching jobs available to foreign teachers in Thailand, both at commercial language centres and within the state system. Such is the demand for teachers that visitors often include teaching English as part of their itinerary for a trip to Thailand. Would-be-teachers do though need training and as a result of there has been a dramatic rise in the number of English teacher training courses available in the Kingdom. Whether it's short courses that give you the basics, or detailed internationally recognized courses that offer a stepping stone into the English teaching profession, there is certainly a course in Thailand to meet your needs.

English though is not the only language you can study in Thailand. As the country takes its place on the international stage, its influence grows around the world. Increasingly, people take Thai language lessons for business and educational purposes, or simply build a short language course into their stay in the country for fun. As a result, a number of commercial Thai language centres catering for expatriates and visitors have emerged to give people an insight into the language.

Of course, with the rise of tourism to Thailand the world is now interested in all things Thai - particularly Thai food. There is an abundance of centres in Thailand teaching foreigners the intricacies of preparing Thai cuisine... and very popular they are, too! With the worldwide boom in Spas and 'Wellness', the demand for masseurs able to offer Thai massage is increasing and the number of visitors studying massage in Thailand growing. Likewise, more and more visitors take courses in traditional Thai medicine to become practitioners in their own countries.

Cultural and Educational Tourism in Russia

Russia is a country of richest history and culture. The most different religious and cultural traditions of numerous nationalities living there have coexisted from time immemorial.The architectural ensemble of Moscow Kremlin, palaces of Saint Petersburg, and ancient cities of the Golden Ring are known all over the world.

Moscow is the capital of the Russian Federation, and the business, scientific, cultural and tourist centre of Russia.

The first mention of Moscow dates back to 1147. The city was founded by Suzdal prince Jury Dolgoruky (Long-armed). Fast development of Moscow was promoted by its favorable geographical position at a crossing of major trading ways, between the rivers Oka and Volga on the Moskva-river. The architectural shape of the capital city has been formed for centuries.

Best Russian and foreign architects and artists worked in Moscow to create its unique image. Today Moscow is one of the most beautiful capitals in the world. Unique flavour is given to the city by the architectural complex of the Moscow Kremlin, the majestic domes of Vasily the Blessed cathedral, the restored Temple of Christ the Savior, New Maiden Convent, Don's and St. Daniel's monasteries, the palace-and-park ensembles of Kolomenskoe, Kuskovo and Ostankino.

Moscow is a cultural centre of global value. There are more than 70 theatres here, the best known of them the Bolshoi Theatre. Richest collections of painting, graphic art and sculpture are gathered in nearly hundred museums, among them the well-known Tretyakov picture gallery and the Museum of fine arts named after Pushkin. There are scores of concert halls, cinemas and expo-centers in the city.

Today's Moscow is a city of congresses, forums, festivals, industrial exhibitions and fairs, including the Moscow international film festival and the International tourist exhibition MITT.

A visit to the Russian capital gives lots of unforgettable and bright impressions to each and every tourist.The environs of Moscow are also a whole world of cultural, historical and natural monuments. About 2200 tourist sights are officially registered and taken under protection by the state. The towns of Sergiev Posad, Zvenigorod (Ringing City), Serpukhov and Kolomna - situated near Moscow - attract more and more travelers every year.

Among the attractions of the Moscow area, a special place belongs to monasteries which for ages were spiritual centers of the country. The architectural complexes of Trinity-Sergiev's Lavra, New-Jerusalem or Joseph-Volokolamsk monasteries are of just unequalled beauty. And the manors situated near Moscow-Arkhangelskoye, Marphino, Abramtsevo, Sukhanovo, Melikhovo - are both picturesque and romantic.

The Golden Ring of Russia is the most popular tourist route which goes from Moscow to the northeast through old Russian towns: Sergiev Posad, Pereyaslavl-Zalessky, Rostov, Yaroslavl', Uglich, Kostroma, Suzdal', Vladimir and many other. There travelers will see scores of most interesting monuments of architecture and history of XII - XVII centuries.

Walls and towers of fortresses and monasteries, earthen banks, white-stone temples and masterpieces of wooden architecture, unique frescos and icons - all of these witnesses to the centuries passed preserve the unbreakable connection of the Golden Ring cities and allow one to see their common features, and to feel the soul of the ancient Rus'.

The route around the Golden Ring involves some monuments of history and culture included in the UNESCO World Heritage List: the ensemble of Trinity-Sergiev's Lavra, the masterpieces of white-stone architecture in Vladimir and Suzdal'.

The towns of the Golden Ring attract tourists with ancient Russian national crafts. They are Rostov enamel and painted trays from Zhostovo, varnished caskets from Palekh and crystal wares of Gus'-Khrustalny (Goose-the-Crystal) glass-blowers. Traditions of ancient masters pass from generation to generation.

Everyone who loves Russian culture and art or interested in ancient Russian life should visit the Museum of wooden architecture and country life in Suzdal', the house-museum of artist Levitan in Plyos, and the museum Library of Russian Vodka in Uglich.

Historical and cultural monuments of the Vladimir region are incorporated into the tourist route Small Golden Ring. In addition to the cities of Vladimir and Suzdal', it includes other ancient Russian towns: Murom, Gus'-Khrustalny, Aleksandrov, Yuryev-Pol'sky, and Bogol'ubovo (God-loving) where at the confluence of the rivers the Nerl' and the Kl'az'ma - one of the most known monuments of old Russian stone architecture - the Church of Intercession on the Nerl' is situated.

Northern Palmira, Northern Venice, the City of White Nights... It has a lot of beautiful names, that majestic city of Saint Petersburg, perhaps the most beautiful of all Russian cities! The Winter Palace, the spike of the Admiralty proudly shot up in the sky, the Spit of Vasilievsky island, St. Isaac and Kazan cathedrals, the Bronze Horseman, sculptures and most elegant railing of Letniy Sad (Summer Garden), canals and bridges on the Neva raised at night, treasures of the Hermitage and Russian Museum, Mariinsky Opera Theater, and unforgettable midnight sun - all these are features of the city. Saint Petersburg was the native place and cradle of Alexander Pushkin and Fyodor Dostoyevsky, Alexander Block and Anna Akhmatova. This city may be admired indefinitely!

The environs of Saint Petersburg are full of charm as well. You will never get tired of feasting your eyes upon the palaces and parks of Tsarskoe Selo, fountains of Peterhof, or alleys of Pavlovsk where well-known musical evenings were held, including concerts of "the King of Waltz" Johann Strauss.

The Silver Ring of Russia is the tourist route from Saint Petersburg through the northwest area, covering old Russian cities of Novgorod and Pskov, museum-reserve Pushkinskiye Gory (Pushkin Hills), and the cities of Ivangorod, Gdov and Porkhov with their ancient fortresses.

Among historical and architectural monuments of this route a special place belongs to Novgorod Kremlin with its magnificent temples of XI - XV centuries.

The land of the Republic of Karelia to the north of Saint Petersburg is also rich in monuments of culture. The most important of them are the village of Kizhi - the largest in Russia architectural ensemble of national wooden architecture - and Valaam monastery, one of the spiritual centres of Russia established in XIV century on island Valaam in Ladoga lake.

Solovetskie islands with their Spaso-Preobrazhensky monastery having rich and complex history are often called a gem of the White Sea area and the pride of Russian North. Beautiful are the tourist centers in the north of Russia: the cities of Vologda, Arkhangelsk and Kargopol', and the well-known Kirillo-Belozersky Monastery where a most valuable collection of XV - XVIII centuries icons is kept.

The Volga-Mother, the great Russian river! It is a heroine of ancient legends (bylinas) and songs, an integral part of the image and spirit of Russia. Since olden days, the Volga was a major trading way. The cities founded on its banks, in different centuries, in due course have turned into large cultural centers of Russia.

Introduction to the Volga region frequently starts with Kostroma. This old Russian city, a gem of church architecture, is among the main tourist centers of the Golden Ring.

At the confluence of the Oka and Volga rivers, Nizhny Novgorod (Lower New-City) is located the largest Russian trading, scientific and cultural centre, a city with rich centuries-old history. The famous annual Nizhniy Novgorod Fair with its numerous exhibitions and forums is a specific feature of "Lower". The Nizhniy Novgorod land since long ago has been famous for its national crafts: Khokhloma and Gorodets lacquerware and Gorodets wood carving.

Another major city in the Volga region is Kazan', the capital of the Republic of Tatarstan. It has long and intricate history, and in its architectural monuments - such as Kazan Kremlin - primordially Russian spirit is fancifully bound with unique aroma of the East. Today Kazan is a large cultural center where Russian and Tatar national traditions coexist.

The image of the Middle Volga region is shaped by the old merchant cities of Samara, Saratov and Ulyanovsk (former Simbirsk). The largest cities of the southern Volga region are Volgograd and Astrakhan. Tsaritsyn-Stalingrad-Volgograd during its more than four-century history frequently found itself in the centre of the major events of the Russian social and state life. Quite remarkable is the architectural ensemble of Central Embankment of the city with its majestic memorial on Mamayev Kurgan in honor of Stalingrad defenders.

EDUCATION IN BALI

Bali as educational tourism destination has to follow the goal of education program of government of Republic of Indonesia. At the local level, the local government tourism authorities, universities/colleges and tourism stakeholders will be participate in the process of identifying the appropriate themes to form the framework of educational tourism strategy. In addition, inputs also come from travel agents or tour operator to shape the theme and product package. The implementation of the educational tourism in Bali will be based on the existing frameworks of institutions. They provide Bali a more co-coordinated approach to negotiations and strengthen their bargaining position in international market. Creating a neighbor countries market is important because in 2008 almost 67.64 % of tourist flows to Bali resulted from Asia Pacific region where Australia is 15.68% and Japan 18.2% (Bali Government Tourism Office,

2009). Increasing number of foreign tourists visiting Bali should prepare for this new demand. The theme, curriculum, course content and schedule will be the outcome of joint efforts by all stakeholders. To facilitate the delivery of the educational tourism program, tourism stakeholders can take advantage of the University of Udayana as the oldest government university in Bali.

Concerning the projects, external events respectively the project sometimes rise up as a surprise to the project manager and his team. It is essential for the project team to recognize that they must also be responsive to it. It includes the established and latest state-of-the-art technology in which the project is based on, its customers and competitors, its geographical, climatic, social, economic and political settings, in fact, virtually everything that can impact its success. These factors can affect the planning, organizing, staffing and directing which constitute the project manager's main responsibilities.

Bali as an Educational Tourism Destination

Bali which is located in Indonesia is the tourist destination that exist and well known in the world. Bali was named the best island in Asia Pacific and the best spa destination in the world 2009 (DestinAsian and SENSES Magazine, 2009). The number of international tourists arrived in Bali 2008 were 1,968,892 people (Bali Government Tourism Office, 2009). Bali is good destination for learning, leisure and traveling. The attractive of Bali as educational tourism for international students because of three main factors: Bali as international tourist destination, high supported infrastructure, and value for money compare to other countries.

Bali educational tourism is an alternative strategy to the mass tourism developed in Bali. There is also a need of high standard quality of human resource especially in Asia Pacific as this region is growth in industrialization and tourism development. To fulfill this requirement the high and international quality of education and international experience needed. The programs enhance the international understanding between young age's generations that will create the positive image in the future. International education tourism program also help the students to understand the home country and its position in the global context.

Internationally, educational tourism has been recognized as an important market segment in the tourism industry. Although definitions of educational tourism abounds, the best way to conceptualize the market segment is to look at the broad range of activities. These include the classic education-like school trip and study tours (referred to as a model for benign tourism by some scholars, vacation and exchange programs, under and postgraduate study programs, short courses, and language courses.

Expatriates working at overseas universities are also known to arrange compulsory fieldtrips for students during their holidays. Educational tourism programs include international trips and student exchange. The product can be classified into 2 categories: first, the lesson taught in the class with the curriculum based which is part of the formal learning process in the classroom; second, the field trip to special site/place as part the traveling. The later program designed into the learning activities that are not related to the curriculum or discipline.

STUDY TOURISM IN AUSTRALIA

Study tourism in Australia programs provide opportunities to develop skills in the area of tourism that can be applied in many different situations. Australian-Universities.com can be used to locate a program provider to meet your needs and this can be used by international students wanting information about studying tourism in Australia as part of a study abroad Australia program.

Study tourism in Australia means tapping into one of Australia's largest and fastest growing industries. Australian tourism schools are meeting the challenge to provide highly-skilled and competent personnel to work in the tourism industry both in Australia and around the world. For the student this means a well-rounded education with a range of skills applicable in many different employment situations.

Education in Australia

Education in Australia is primarily the responsibility of the states and territories. Each state or territory government provides funding and regulates the public and private schools within its governing area. The federal government helps fund the public universities, but is not involved in setting curriculum. Generally, education in Australia follows the three-tier model which includes primary education (primary schools), followed by secondary education (secondary schools/high schools) and tertiary education (universities and/or TAFE Colleges).

The Programme for International Student Assessment (PISA) 2006 evaluation ranked the Australian education system as 6th for Reading, 8th for Science and 13th for Mathematics, on a worldwide scale including 56 countries. The Education Index, published with the UN's Human Development Index in 2008, based on data from 2006, lists Australia as 0.993, amongst the highest in the world, tied for first with Denmark & Finland.

Education in Australia is compulsory between the ages of five and fifteen to seventeen, depending on the state or territory, and date of birth. Post-compulsory education is regulated within the Australian Qualifications Framework, a unified system of national qualifications in schools, vocational education and training (TAFE) and the higher education sector (university).

The academic year in Australia varies between states and institutions, but generally runs from late January/early February until mid-December for primary and secondary schools, with slight variations in the inter-term holidays and TAFE colleges, and from late February until mid-November for universities with seasonal holidays and breaks for each educational institute.

Pre-school

Pre-school (also known as Kindergarten in some states and territories) in Australia is relatively unregulated, and is not compulsory. The first exposure many Australian children have to learn with others outside of traditional parenting is day care or a parent-run playgroup. This sort of activity is not generally considered schooling, as Pre-school education is separate from primary school in all states and territories, except Western Australia and Queensland where pre-school education is taught as part of the primary school system.

Pre-schools are usually run by the State and Territory Governments, except in Victoria, South Australia and New South Wales where they are run by local councils, community groups or private organisations. Pre-school is offered to three- to five-year-olds; attendance numbers vary widely between the states, but 85.7% of children attended pre-school the year before school. The year before a child is due to attend primary school is the main year for pre-school education. This year is far more commonly attended, and may take the form of a few hours of activity during weekdays.

Responsibility for pre-schools in New South Wales and Victoria, lies with the Department of Community Services and the Department of Human Services, respectively. In all other states and territories of Australia, responsibility for pre-schools lie with the relevant education department.

School

School education in Australia is compulsory between certain ages as specified by state or territory legislation. Depending on the state or territory, and date of birth of the child, school is compulsory from the age of five to six to the age of fifteen to seventeen. In recent years, over three quarters of students stay at school until they are seventeen. Government schools educate approximately 65% of Australian students, with approximately 34% in Catholic and Independent schools. A small portion of students are legally home-schooled, particularly in rural areas.

Government schools (also known as public schools) are free to attend for Australian citizens and permanent residents, while Catholic and Independent schools usually charge attendance fees. However in addition to attendance fees; stationery, textbooks, uniforms, school camps and other schooling costs are not covered under government funding. The additional cost for schooling has been estimated to be on average $316 per year per child.

Regardless of whether a school is part of the Government, Catholic or Independent systems, they are required to adhere to the same curriculum frameworks of their state or territory. The curriculum framework however provides for some flexibility in the syllabus, so that subjects such as religious education can be taught. Most school students wear uniforms, although there are varying expectations and some Australian schools do not require uniforms. A common movement among secondary schools to support student voice has taken form as organisations such as VicSRC in Victoria bring together student leaders to promote school improvement.

CATHOLIC AND INDEPENDENT SCHOOLS

Catholic schools enroll 20.2% of students, while non-Catholic non-government schools, often called Independent schools, enroll 13.7% of students.

Most Catholic schools are either run by their local parish, local diocese and their state's Catholic Education Department. Independent schools include schools operated by secular educational philosophies such as Montessori, however, the majority of Independent schools are religious, being Protestant, Jewish, Islamic or non-denominational.

Some Catholic and Independent schools charge high fees, because of this Government funding for these schools often comes under criticism from the Australian Education Union and the Australian Labor Party.

Common Ages

Students may be slightly younger or older than stated below, due to variation between states and territories. The name for the first year of Primary school varies considerably between states and territories, e.g. what is known as Kindergarten in ACT and NSW may mean the year preceding the first year of primary school or preschool in other states and territories. Some states vary in whether Year 7 is part of the Primary or Secondary years, as well as the existence of a middle school system.

Primary

- Kindergarten (QLD) 3-4 year olds
- Pre-school / Kindergarten / Prep (ACT, NT, NSW and SA/ TAS, VIC and WA / QLD): 4-5 year olds
- Kindergarten / Preparatory / Pre-Primary / Reception / Transition(ACT and NSW / TAS, VIC and QLD / WA / SA / NT): 5-6 year olds
- Year 1: 6-7 year olds
- Year 2: 7-8 year olds
- Year 3: 8-9 year olds
- Year 4: 9-10 year olds

- Year 5: 10-11 year olds
- Year 6: 11-12 year olds
- Year 7: 12-13 year olds (QLD, SA, WA)

Secondary

- Year 7: 12-13 year olds (ACT, NSW, TAS, VIC) (Middle School NT)
- Year 8: 13-14 year olds
- Year 9: 14-15 year olds
- Year 10: 15-16 year olds (High School NT)
- Year 11: 16-17 year olds
- Year 12: 17-19 year olds

Comparison of ages and Year levels across States and Territories

Students can undertake Year 12 for up to three years, students who complete Year 12 under a reduced work load generally do this in two years, this is usually referred to "Year 13".

Year(s) In School	1	2	3	4	5	6	7	8	9	10	11	12	13
Australian Capital Territory	Primary School							High School				College	
	Kindergarten	Year 1	Year 2	Year 3	Year 4	Year 5	Year 6	Year 7	Year 8	Year 9	Year 10	Year 11	Year 12
New South Wales	Primary School							High School					
	Kindergarten	Year 1	Year 2	Year 3	Year 4	Year 5	Year 6	Year 7	Year 8	Year 9	Year 10	Year 11	Year 12
Northern Territory	Primary School							Middle School			High School		
	Transition	Year 1	Year 2	Year 3	Year 4	Year 5	Year 6	Year 7	Year 8	Year 9	Year 10	Year 11	Year 12

Queensland	Primary School								High School				
	Preparatory	Year 1	Year 2	Year 3	Year 4	Year 5	Year 6	Year 7	Year 8	Year 9	Year 10	Year 11	Year 12
South Australia	Junior primary school			Primary school					Secondary School/High School				
	Reception	Year 1	Year 2	Year 3	Year 4	Year 5	Year 6	Year 7	Year 8	Year 9	Year 10	Year 11	Year 12
Tasmania	Primary School							High School				College	
	Preparatory	Grade 1	Grade 2	Grade 3	Grade 4	Grade 5	Grade 6	Year 7	Year 8	Year 9	Year 10	Year 11	Year 12
Victoria	Primary School							Secondary School				VCE	
	Preparatory	Grade 1	Grade 2	Grade 3	Grade 4	Grade 5	Grade 6	Year 7	Year 8	Year 9	Year 10	Year 11	Year 12
Western Australia	Primary School								High School				
	Pre-	Year	Year	Year	Year	Year	Year	Yea	Yea	Yea	Yea	Yea	Yea

In the Northern Territory, primary schools often include a pre-school. In Western Australia, primary schools often include two pre-school years.

Children that have been identified as gifted may begin school earlier than the stated minimum age in some states and territories. Additionally gifted students may 'skip' a subject or year and advance to a higher grade in schooling.

Tertiary

Tertiary education (or higher education) in Australia is primarily study at University or a Technical college in order to receive a qualification or further skills and training.

Federal Department

Education in Australia has been the responsibility of the following departments:

- Department of Education, Employment and Training (DEET) (1987)
- Department of Employment, Education, Training and Youth Affairs (DEETYA) (1996)
- Department of Education, Training and Youth Affairs (DETYA) (1997)
- Department of Education, Science and Training (DEST) (2001)
- Department of Education, Employment and Workplace Relations (DEEWR) (2007)

VICTORIAN CERTIFICATE OF EDUCATION

The Victorian Certificate of Education or VCE is the credential awarded to secondary school students who successfully complete high school level studies (Year 11 and 12 or equivalent) in the state of Victoria, Australia. Study for the VCE is usually completed over two years, but it can be spread over a longer period in some cases. It is possible to pass and obtain the VCE without completing the end of year exams. The VCE was established in 1987, replacing the earlier Higher School Certificate (HSC).

Structure of the VCE

The Victorian Certificate of Education is generally taught in Year 11 and 12 of secondary college in Victoria, however some students commence their VCE studies in Year 10 or earlier if the school allows it.

All VCE studies are organised into units (VCE subjects typically consist of four units; each unit covers one semester of study). Each unit comprises a set number of outcomes (usually two or three); an outcome describes the knowledge and skills that a student should demonstrate by the time the student has completed the unit.

Subject choice depends on each individual school. Unit 3/4 of a subject must be studied in sequential order, whereas Unit 1/2 can be mixed and matched. Students are not required to complete all the units of a subject as part of the VCE course, meaning they are able to change subject choice between Year 11 and Year 12.

On completing a unit, a student receives either a 'satisfactory' (S) or 'non-satisfactory' (N) result. If a student does not intend to proceed to tertiary education, a 'satisfactory' result is all that is required to graduate with the VCE. If a student does wish to study at a tertiary level then they will require an ATAR. In order to gain an ATAR a student must satisfactorily complete three units of any subject in the English field (at least one English field subject is compulsory) and sixteen units in any other subjects.

ASSESSMENT

VCE studies are assessed both internally (in school) and externally (through VCAA). During Unit 1/2 all assessment is internal, whilst in Unit 3/4 assessment is conducted both internally and externally.

Internal Assessment

Internal assessment is conducted via "school assessed coursework" (SACs) and "school assessed tasks" (SATs).

"School assessed coursework" (SACs) are the primary avenue of internal assessment, with assessment in every VCE study consisting of at least one SAC. SACs are tasks that are written by the school and must be done primarily in class time; they can include essays, reports, tests, and case studies. Some studies in the visual arts and technology areas are also assessed via "school assessed tasks" (SATs). SATs are generally practical tasks that are examined in school. Both

SACs and SATs are scaled by VCAA against external assessment; this is to eliminate any cheating or variances in task difficulty.

External Assessment

External assessment is conducted in the form of examinations set by the Victorian Curriculum and Assessment Authority for Unit 3/4 studies. Midyear (June) examinations are held for all subjects in the Science field, as well as accounting. End of year (October/November) examinations are held for all studies.

Subjects in the LOTE field are also assessed in the form of oral examinations. Subjects in the Music field are assessed by a performance for a VCAA panel of examiners as part of their external assessment. All performance based external assessment (Oral Examinations and Music Performances) are typically held in early October.

GENERAL ACHIEVEMENT TEST (GAT)

The GAT is an essential part of VCE external assessment. It provides the basis of a quality assurance check on the marking of examinations. Any student who is enrolled in a VCE Unit 3/4 study is expected to sit the GAT.

Scoring

Study Scores

A student who satisfactorily completes Unit 3/4 of a VCE study is eligible for a study score of between 0 and 50. Study scores are calculated by VCAA and indicate a students performance in that subject relative to others.

Study scores are calculated according to a normal distribution, where the mean is 30 and the standard deviation is 7.

Scaling

Scaling is the process that adjusts VCE study scores into ATAR subject scores. The Victorian Tertiary Admissions Centre (VTAC) adjusts all VCE study scores to equalise results in more difficult studies with those in easier subjects. Scaling down occurs when the overall performance is high. Scaling up happens when the overall performance is low.

Enter

VCE Studies

In total there are 129 VCE studies ranging across education fields including humanities, science, mathematics, technology, the arts and language as well as incorporating vocational studies.

- A student must study an English subject; with a choice between English, English (ESL), English Language or English Literature; Literature is regarded as the most difficult English subject. Approximately 75% of students study English, rather than the other three options.
- Mathematics. At Unit 1 and 2 level a student may study Foundation Mathematics, General Mathematics or Mathematical Methods (CAS). At Unit 3 and 4 a student may study Further Mathematics (practical application - data analysis and discrete mathematics), Mathematical Methods (CAS) (mainstream calculus based course) or Specialist Mathematics (advanced calculus based course). Specialist Mathematics requires concurrent or previous study of Mathematical Methods/ Mathematical Methods (CAS) at the Unit 3 and 4 level

CHAPTER–2

GROWTH AND DEVELOPMENT

Travellers have always been met with hospitality. Modern western practice might place this on a commercial, cafe-type footing which would feel rather distant to many cultures around the globe, but it is still the rule. We want to treat visitors as we would ourselves hope to be treated. Once the need for food and shelter are satisfied the task is to help fulfil the reason for the visit. Family ties are rehearsed, news exchanged. The business of the day is carried out. Leisure activity is enjoyed. Having explored the personal, the place can be examined. The host can show the guest their house or premises.

Given time and occasion the visitor can be shown around the neighbourhood. It will be important to the host to pick out what is special or unusual for the guest. What is different will be of interest. Perhaps the local architecture has a different style through shapes and materials. Trees, shrubs and plants might contrast with the visitor's home environment. Are there domestic or wild animals which are unusual? How do people get around - on foot, or using animals or some form of transport? How do people behave, relate to each other and carry out the necessary tasks of daily life? Are all these things just the same as at home or very different, and why? Above all, what has been the importance of the new place in terms of the people and events which have occupied it?

Those folk who are visiting their relatives and friends will have the answers to these questions ready at hand. Or, like Paula the Roman lady in the previous posting they may have hired a guide or joined a whole group for a conducted tour. The nice thing about humans is that you can ask questions. The problem might be that they are too few or too expensive to be enjoyed. The ancient Roman Empire meant that many people were attracted to Rome and its historic places. Its churches were popular for visitors and would, for some, require longer visits than others, especially if time was to be spent in contemplation or worship. So all these factors encouraged a demand for some other form of information to be available, and it could be satisfied by books. Hand written on papyrus or vellum, they were not like later mass productions and they would be expensive, but for those who could afford them the guide book was beginning to appear.

Around 610AD a guide book could be bought to the churches of Rome. The 'Notitia ecclesiarium urbis Romae' was more of a listing for church authorities of what pilgrims were already visiting. It might have worked like market research in a way, showing which buildings and monuments were of greatest interest. A slightly later guide was written for visitors. It began rather than ended at St Peter's like its predecessor, gave a wider description of the city and according to Nicholas T Parsons (2007:86) was more colourful, claiming for example "that an altar in St Peter's was made by the saint himself; and that a rock kept in the oratory of St Stephen the Protomartyr on the Ostia road was used in his stoning".

Famous sailor Christopher Columbus was not the first European to reach the Americas. Leif Ericson sailed to Newfoundland in 1001 AD. Nor were those continental regions named after him. That distinction belongs possibly to either Amerigo Vespucci who explored the coasts of South America between 1497 and 1504, or to Richard Ameryk who was the principal owner of the ship that John Cabot, the English explorer, used to sail to North America in 1497. It was Martin Waldseemüller who named the Americas in his world map of 1507, using information about Vespucci and Ameryk, not all of which was necessarily genuine.

So why are the continents not named after Ericson - North and South Ericsonia? The answer is that Ericson's journey was did not have the impact on European knowledge that Columbus had. The Genoese explorer had spent time trying to raise money and get support for an Atlantic crossing in order to pioneer a western route to South East Asia and hopefully to discover lands that would repay his backers and bring riches to whichever monarch supported him. He therefore had created a measure of knowledge about himself before the voyage. Even more important was the quite deliberate publicity that he fostered on his return. This brought him to the attention of royalty and geographers alike at a time when Europeans were absorbed in a great age of exploration and colonisation. Voyages and land expeditions of discovery were being made around Africa and into Asia at a time of intense rivalry. In Ericson's time, five hundred years before, there was little interest in such things as European kings had more pressing concerns within their continent and towards the Holy Land.

Columbus made four voyages across the Atlantic. The third and fourth reached the coast of what we call South America and Central America respectively, but none involved North America. In this however he had already outperformed Leif Ericson's single voyage.

Columbus had, after several years' attempts, finally obtained a contract with Queen Isabella and King Ferdinand of Castile and Aragon which gave him permission to go and which funded his travels. In return Isabella hoped for financial gain and the chance of colonies. The explorer had the intention of reaching the Indies - South and South East Asia - with their riches of spice and other commodities. He believed from his reading of the maps and scientific thought of the time that the journey would have been smaller than it actually is. On finding land on his first voyage he decided these were the Indies. On the later realisation that this was a very different set of islands the area took on the label 'the West Indies'.

When he got back to Spain Columbus wrote letters detailing his discovery and sent them to officials in the governments of Castile and of Aragon, with another to the Pope. These were important letters in terms of politics as well as his own position and hopes of further voyages. The letter to Luis de Santangel, the Finance Minister of Aragon, was passed by him to a printer in Barcelona who made copies for immediate distribution. The text was in Latin. It was a popular document: by the end of the same year, 1493, nine editions had been run off and printers in Paris, Antwerp, Basel and Florence had produced copies.

By 1500 over 3,000 copies had circulated throughout Europe, a very large printing for those days of what was the first popular eyewitness travel account. Printing 'by movable type' as it is known and that was responsible for the ability to circulate so much information so quickly had only been available for a few decades. But it allowed Martin Waldseemüller and other cartographers to know of the discoveries and incorporate something about them into their new maps. It allowed authors to report and speculate further on the discoveries and their significance for the people of the age.

How do you know that Australia exists? Maybe when you were young your great uncle told you he wrestled goannas along Christmas Creek on the Gulf of Carpentaria when he worked as a bandicoot farmer. Did you believe him?

Or perhaps there was that TV series called Skippy the Bush Kangaroo or the movie 'Australia' with Hugh Jackman. Or did you take your lead on all things Oz from that geography teacher who lived for six months in Melbourne and reckoned it the best, the only important city on the continent. As you finished your days as a student you decided New Zealand was the place to be because Australia was full of men with corks hanging from their bush hats, swigging Fosters and decrying the chance of pommie bastards ever learning to play cricket.

Then your best friend wanted to spend a gap year in Sydney, had the offer of a house to stay in and a bar job to take up. And wanted you to join them - jobs available, fun to be had - so you went.

So you learned out there that you wouldn't farm bandicoots, not even larrikins dangle corks from their hats and the neighbours in Sydney prefer baseball. You never did have doubts about Australia existing .... but what the place was really like, what sort of people lived there and how different everyday life was from that back home - or just how similar it was - you only found out by being a kind of working tourist. You went to see for yourself. Then you understood better because you saw things first hand, saw them for yourself.

It was an education. Not school-style, but through real life encounters with people and places. Out there you travelled as much as you could, up to the Great Barrier Reef and into the Snowy Mountains. You saw a sheep station, a kangaroo, some of the most beautiful sea life on the planet and the Sydney Harbour Bridge. As it happened those neighbours out there had only seen the Bridge, none of those other things, because they liked their city, spent Saturday washing the car and mowing the lawn and Sunday went to the beach. They had heard of those other places but would rather stay at home and see them on the telly. They had never been tourists, a phenomenon that you hadn't thought possible - people who never went anywhere outside their home town.

DEVELOPMENT OF EDUCATIONAL TOURISM

385 AD

St Jerome records the visit of travellers to Jerusalem. They are shown places with Biblical associations. A Roman lady, Paula, takes away pebbles from some of the sites, reads aloud from a Bible, and shows great emotions at Calvary.

Pope Damasius arranges for a signposting system to be installed in the catacombs of Rome.

c610

Pilgrims to Rome are able to buy a guide to a route around the main churches of Rome. The term "pilgrim" derives from the Latin "peregrinus" meaning foreigner or stranger, and by association becomes for a time a general word meaning traveller.

c850

The supposed body of St James the Apostle is "discovered" at Compostela in north-west Spain. A shrine is built and he becomes known there as St James of Compostela.

1279

The monastery of St Maximin in Provence claims to have the body of Mary Magdalene in a sarcophagus. The Count of Provence holds a gala ceremony to display the relic and Pope Boniface VIII grants an indulgence on it. The cathedral of Vezelay in Burgundy had long claimed to have the body, but its boast was soon discounted in favour of St Maximin.

c13 C

The journey to Rome is made by the Church into part of a credit system towards so many years of pardon for sins: eg one journey followed by 395 high masses gives ninety-two years' pardon.

1394

First licence is issued to an English 'pilgrim shipper' to sail from Plymouth to La Corunna, taking pilgrims travelling to Compostela. The journey took four days' sailing and a few hours' walk.

By 1428

925 pilgrim boats are operating from England to Spain. They often returned with wine as an additional cargo.

1572

Sir Philip Sydney commences a Grand Tour, paid for by Queen Elizabeth I, in order to learn continental methods of government. Returns in 1575.

Sydney visits bi-annual Frankfurt Book Fair, an international gathering of publishers, scholars and authors. The city population tripled during that time. The Book Fair is still held.

1591

Fynes Moryson sets out on a Grand Tour paid for by Queen Elizabeth I, to study law, and also receives £20 for each of two years from Peterhouse College, Cambridge - about £1,000 per year at 1980 prices.

1620

(May) First known 'Herbarizing' excursion organised by the Society of Apothecaries, when apprentices were taught to recognise the 'simples' or drug plants during a visit to the country. The Society later appointed a 'Demonstrator of

Plants' who stood in the Chelsea Physic Garden on the last Wednesday in each month to expound the names of plants. Herbarizings finally ceased in 1834 when it was decided that London had grown too big to organise practicable excursions.

1661

Samuel Pepys records a visit to Hatfield House and a guided tour by the Earl of Shaftesbury's gardener.

1670

First use of the term 'Grand Tour'.

1689

The Temple Coffee House Botanic Club is formed as a social group meeting on Friday evenings, with excursions on Sundays and some summer holidays to places round London.

1699

Joseph Addison sets out on a Grand Tour to write a new guidebook to Europe based on the writings of Horace and Virgil.

1750

Cost of lodging in Rome, per week, £4 (? £100 at modern prices). Cost of three-volume guidebook to Rome, Antica and Moderna, 10/- (1980 prices ? £13.50).

1773

The 'Annual Register' classifies the reasons for foreign travel as "polite education, the love of variety, the pursuit of health" (cf 1768).

1832

William Buckland, Reader in Geology at Oxford, holds one of his famous "Geological Rides" for the British Association meeting in Oxford. Meets in carriages or on horseback on the London Road and proceed to Shotover Hill where refreshments are taken in tents, fossils are purchased from local labourers, and Buckland lectures.

1835

Adam Sedgwick starts "Geological Rides" from Cambridge. they prove instantly popular - up to seventy students on horseback follow him across the fens and hear five lectures in a day, the last usually being on fen drainage, delivered on the cathedral roof at Ely.

1839

The first guidebook is published by Baedeker: in due course it will lead to a series of leading European guides.

1841

Thomas Cook's first excursion takes 570 people by train from Leicester to Loughborough for an event in the open air with speeches, entertainment and food. Cook's purpose is stated to be "to unite man with man, and man with God" (Cook's "Physical, Moral and Social Aspects of Excursions and Tours"). The event is notable for the quality and detail of the arrangements.

1845

Thomas Cook organises a public trip to Liverpool which does not have any motive other than to have an enjoyable time - ie the 1841 excursion was aimed at promoting teetotalism. Cook checks all hotels and restaurants in advance for his 350 participants. Afterwards he writes a "Handbook of the Trip to Liverpool" - the first guidebook of its kind. As this tour included transport, meals, accommodation and 'the services of a tour manager' as we would now say, it qualifies as the first-ever leisure package tour, over a century before the first aircraft-based trips to the Mediterranean. The previous Loughborough visit was a day excursion only.

1854

Thomas Cook's first European Tour.

1865

Thomas Cook's first tour of the USA.

1872

Thomas Cook's first world tour.

Foundation of the Polytechnic Touring Association under the influence of Quentin Hogg.

1891

The Reverend T A Leonard takes a party from Colne in Ambleside for four days at a cost of 21/- a head. This leads to the formation of the Co-operative Holidays Association as a company in 1897.

1897

The CHA puts funds into starting the Free Holiday Movement, with members nominating poor people for free holidays. The following year the CHA refers to members as "Sons of Faith, Nature and Comradeship".

1907

An Act of Parliament is passed setting up the National Trust in its present form.

Richard Schirmann, in Germany, opens his school to slum children, and begins the "wandervogel" movement. It is anti-militarist, anti-machinery, pro country life. The origins of youth hostelling are usually traced to this date, though the Swedish Touring Club had provided low-cost accommodation in simple shelters.

Baden-Powell's first scout camp is held on Brownsea Island in Poole Harbour from 9 August. Of twenty boys taking part, nine were members of the Boys' Brigade. In September, Robert Young forms a Glasgow Schools' Officer Training Corps, and is later persuaded by Baden-Powell to introduce Scout training.

1908

The Boy Scouts' Movement is begun officially by Baden-Powell. "Scouting for Boys" begins to be issued fortnightly at 4d a copy from January. In May, the first Scout Camp is held by a Sunderland troop under Colonel Vaux, camping for a month. Many participants were newsboys and received 5/- a week from Colonel Vaux to cover lost earnings. Halfway through they were joined by the Kangaroo Patrol of the 1st Hampstead Troop.

1919

Steve Mather of US National Parks Service observes Lake Tahoe Guides interpreting the area to visitors. Their organisers, Mr and Mrs Goethe, had drawn inspiration from a British field teacher using heuristic methods at the Lake of the Four Cantons in Switzerland.

1920

The Order of Woodcraft Chivalry founded by Ernest Westlake. It will use outdoor activities as an educational strategy - similar to the Boy Scouts and other movements.

1920

Horace M Albright of the US National Parks Service hires a Park Ranger to give lectures, guided walks and field trips, produce a bulletin and operate a museum. He later recalls that in the early 1900s interpretive techniques were in use at Yosemite, Yellowstone, and in Arizona.

1940

Gordonstoun School is evacuated to Plas Dinan, Merionethshire for the duration of the war. Kurt Hahn obtains financial help from Lawrence holt of the Blue Funnel Line to start the Outward Bound school at Aberdovey, which he does in the following year. His Moray Badge scheme of character training had been tried by local authorities under the title of the County Badge scheme, but it was not successful until modified as the Duke of Edinburgh's Award post-war. Hahn's wish to pursue adventure training was directed into the Aberdovey venture meanwhile.

c 1940 HMI Schools Inspector Francis Butler identifies the cultural gap between urban and rural children, as shown during the evacuation. He joins with Professor Wooldridge in advocating field studies.

1941

Aberdovey Outward Bound School opens: first purpose-built educational centre to concentrate on education within the countryside.

1946

The first Field Studies Centre is opened at Flatford Mill in Suffolk.

1950

White Hall, Derbyshire County Council's country pursuits centre, opens near Buxton. Main drive behind it is Sir Jack Longland, who had been on the 1933 Everest Expedition, was on the Board of the Outward Bound Trust and had connections with Abbotsholme.

GRAND TOUR TO EDUCATE PEOPLE

Tourism was used at key points in British history to educate people. It is possible to argue that it was filling an educational role most of the time, at least in its early stages. Virtually all forms of tourism began for educational reasons. Most currently available work underplays this fact, with the possible exception of discussions on the Grand Tour. Holloway (1989, p179) makes a statement about "tourists and locals alike widening their horizons" almost as an afterthought to a short discussion of sociocultural problems. Cooper et al refer to myths surrounding tourism which "should be broken", pointing out "Tourism is not purely for the purposes of leisure.

It also includes business tourism, pilgrimages and tourism for health purposes" (Cooper et al, 1993, p1). A later chapter on "The Future of Tourism" makes only passing mention to `new' tourists looking for "rewarding activities to fill their leisure time and to satisfy their cultural, intellectual and sporting interests", but it is only in the context of the needs of certain market segments in "multi-interest travel". Voase (1995) in an interesting and useful book touches on many aspects of tourism which relate to education, without dealing with it as a perspective. A chapter about the future discusses economics, global warming, people in tourism, sustainability, transport and fashions, but not tourism as an educative activity.

Ryan's "The Chase of a Dream, the End of a Play" (in Ryan, 1997, p23) refers to tourism as an educative process within the context of sociological discussion. The historical references consider tourism largely as leisure and escapism. Hollinshead's "Heritage Tourism Under Post-modernity: Truth and the Past" in the same collection as Ryan (1997), shows how great a gap there is between the sociological critic on the one hand and the teacher of history on the other, as the scholarship of Samuel's "Theatres of Memory" (1994) illustrates. Hollinshead paints a pessimistic picture of a world in which all history teaching outside the classroom or library appears impossible since it long ago succumbed to a conspiracy by various forces of darkness.

There is little illumination in this kind of writing for the history teacher working out of the classroom. History teachers know well that all interpretations - including books and academic papers - of the world take particular viewpoints, selecting, interpreting and presenting reality as they see it. Even so, a re-assessment of tourism which hopes to be accepted at a higher academic level will have to establish a credible, theoretical and practical counter-argument to the Hollinshead kind of view.

Weiler and Hall edited a collection of papers in "Special Interest Tourism" (1992) which look at a number of case studies and review some sectors. They point to the "diversity of market segments and products ... encompassed within the rubric of `special interest tourism'" and "the limited amount of research that has been done". The book unfortunately suffers from being more a collection of snapshots of relevant areas, but the opening chapter does attempt an overview. Sadly, it remains only a collection of separate perspectives such as marketing, ethics and green tourism, rather than shining a well-focused new light on the whole issue.

Within the book, the paper on "Educational Travel" is particularly disappointing in its attempt to take a historical perspective. It makes only two references, the first to the Grand Tour as the originator of educational travel and second to 'Chautauqua'. "The modem-day learning vacation concept seems to have originated at Chautauqua, a residential institution in New York.

Initiated in 1874 by a Methodist minister and an Ohio businessman, Chautauqua blends the concept of an outdoor recreation setting with social activities and learning opportunities" (Kalinowski and Weiler, 1992). This American example is interesting and important as it led to some 12,000 similar centres within the United States, but they were largely centres where general educational activities took place, rather than centres where people discovered their (temporary) new environments through first-hand contact. As a perspective on educational tourism it is disappointing. Another look must be taken at the history of tourism forms.

The pilgrimage was an early form of informal education as it brought devotees closer to knowledge of sacred sites and introduced them to new experiences and knowledge, but not in any didactic way. Prehistoric pilgrimages took place to centres associated with magical properties and religious beliefs, and specifically Christian pilgrimages were undertaken at least from the late fourth century AD. Around 610 AD pilgrims could buy a guide to the churches of Rome - an early aid to visitor interpretation (Feifer, 1985).

The Canterbury Pilgrims, following a well-used route from Winchester or London to Canterbury Cathedral relied on a growing infrastructure of tracks, inns and stables in order to make their journey. In Poland, the monastery of Jasna Gora in Czestochowa, founded in 1382, received thousands of pilgrims each year to see an image of the Blessed Virgin Mary housed there: by 1682 it was around 140,000, and by the present day it sometimes welcomes a million in a single year. Historically, each visit was part of a process of communication and teaching in which what the pilgrims had seen and experienced was fed back to others in their own villages and towns (Jablonski, 1996.

The nature of the Grand Tour as an education for the sons of the English gentry has been well covered (Pimlott 1947, Hibbert 1969, Brodsky-Porges 1981, Hugill 1985, Towner 1985, Feifer 1985, and Adler 1989). Rooted in the explorations of Queen Elizabeth I's age, the Grand Tour was encouraged by her as a means of training men for government. Feifer (1985, p64) quotes James Howell's "Instructions for Forraine Travel" (1642) comparing the stay-at-home with the traveller. "To run over and traverse the world by hearsay ... other men's eyes ... is but a confused and imperfect kind of speculation, which leaveth but weak and distrustful notions" said Howell of the former, and praised the first-hand view of the latter: "the eye ... as through a clear and crystal casement we ... in one instant comprehend half the whole universe".

Though the later Grand Tourists were more interested in pleasure than in being educated, the whole experience remained educational in the widest of senses. Even time spent in a brothel would teach the young buck about life. The part played by Grand Touring in British culture is well documented, but there was an important influence on industry and technology, too see Armytage, 1961 p 96 on the influence of the Canal du Midi on the British Industrial Revolution, and Klingender, 1972, pp 85-86 on de Loutherbourg and dramatic presentation.

Thomas Cook's entry into the history of travelling was made by a desire to educate. The 1841 railway excursion from Leicester to Loughborough took five hundred people to an open space where Cook, a Baptist preacher, could educate them about the evils that he saw in alcohol. However successful he might have been in his chosen aim, he was certainly successful in his method. With a combination of the excitement of open-wagon rail travel, the leisurely nature of the day, and the ambience of a different environment, the Leicester folk must have been in a receptive and tolerant mood. No consumer motivator could ask for more. Thomas Cook's contributions were all about packaging travel, an attention to detail, and the providing of quality experiences, but above all the enjoyment by his customers of discovering new places.

The growth of seaside holidays is also well documented (Walvin 1978, Parry 1983, Stafford and Yates 1985, Ward and

Hardy 1985, Jordan and Jordan 1991, Shaw and Williams 1997). From them it can be seen that even the hedonism of the seaside existed alongside the wonders of discovery. In 1788 Catherine Hutton from Birmingham wrote home about the people she encountered in Blackpool: "The Boltoners are sincere, good humoured and noisy.

The Manchestrians reserved and purse-proud, the Liverpoolians free and open as the ocean upon which they get their riches" (quoted in Walvin, 1978, p31). And while Blackpool was a place of social encounter, it was also one with an Opera House, an Aquarium, a Menagerie, a Winter Gardens with "high class concerts", and its famous Circus. From 1910 even the Pleasure Beach had its "edutainment" in devices like the Naval Spectatorium which used 360-degree film projection and mechanical devices to present representations of the American Civil War, and later, World War I naval battles (Turner and Palmer, 1976). Such devices were the norm for resorts which wanted to entertain their visitors, and indeed, Scarborough retains its "Naval Warfare" event to this day.

Presenting the wonders of the world has been a foundation for entertainment ever since the earliest bards told their stories. In due course the resorts of the industrialised world built fair grounds, theatres, museums, galleries, menageries and gardens drawing upon the culture, artefacts, flora and fauna of the world around them. Fairs like the Kursaal at Southend-on-Sea, Dreamland at Margate, and the Paradium at Great Yarmouth (Pearson, 1991) derived excitement from representations, however distorted, of reality. The huge Coney Island parks in New York almost became international expositions in their own right by building theatres, cinemas and other shows (Snow and Wright, 1976). They were in direct line of descent from the London, Paris, Vienna and Chicago Exhibitions long before Disney.

Visiting great houses and museums, and the educational value that related to such excursions, has been a recent subject of analysis (Tinniswood 1989, Ousby 1990). Ousby says that "Travel was a leading instrument of that post-Reformation spirit of enquiry which valued empirical knowledge over abstract speculation or book-learning derived merely from tradition" (Ousby, 1990).

It was during the middle years of the nineteenth century, and in parallel with the beginnings of formalised education for various age groups from young to old, that the practice was established of townspeople and city dwellers making day visits to the country. These were not only for what we might term `escapist' entertainment, but for `self-improvement'.

Local newspapers of the time are full of the accounts of annual outings by social groups from chapels or work-places (Delgado 1977, Jordan and Jordan 1991). There are detailed accounts preserved of the organisation required for the bigger trips, such as the well-known railway excursions from the Bass Breweries (Pearson, 1993). These show how guide books and visits of an `improving nature' were made integral to the excursions by those who organised them. One quotation from the 40-page booklet distributed to 8,000 participants in the 1914 visit to Scarborough will give a flavour:

"The improvements made since our last visit in 1910 consist of deepening the old or West Harbour by about three to four feet, so as to accommodate and give more room for fishing craft of a larger size and to the increasing number of Steam Drifters now engaged in the Herring Fishery, in addition to the Sailing Herring Fishers. The West Pier, where the fish is landed, sold and packed, has been widened - 70 feet being added - and now provides excellent curing and packing spaces for the herring curers and exporters" (Bass Museum, 1975)

A videotaped account given by a retired worker from John Crossley and Sons' carpet mills in Halifax shows in anecdote some of the cultural effects. Mrs Florence Waite took part in a long railway excursion over 30 hours to Edinburgh, Glasgow and the Isle of Bute in 1934 with Crossley's Social Club. The impact made by Edinburgh's particular historic character, and the Clyde's glorious scenery, are clear even after sixty years (Waite, 1994).

Delgado has shown how important the annual excursion was as an escape from the industrial city. In 1912 the Duchess of Sunderland foresaw "A day that is a glimpse of Paradise to the poor little mites who live in the darkness of squalid back courts and the mean streets of our cities", when raising money for a charity sending children on a countryside excursion (Delgado, 1977).

Thomas Cook had religious motives (it was his son John Mason Cook who went fully commercial in tourism), believing that through his tours "man has been brought nearer to man and nearer to his Creator" (Brendon, 1991). It must be stressed that Cook began as an evangelist, a communicator, and not a tour operator. However unconsciously, he succeeded because he removed his audience from the stress of everyday life, induced within them a receptive and relaxed frame of mind, and then tried to persuade them to adopt a new lifestyle based on Christianity and, in particular, teetotalism. This aligns with Turner's analysis of the pilgrimage with its ideas of separation, liminality and communitas (Turner 1973, 1974: see discussion in Urry, 1990 pp10-11).

But it also aligns with the principles of propaganda and persuasion of the use of group psychology, removing his audience to a different setting, creating a receptive mood and using crowd psychology to persuade individuals to adopt new attitudes (Brown, 1963 and Jowett and O'Donnell, 1992). Cook's Loughborough excursion operated in terms of communication between people, and between people and environments, depending on the contrasts between Leicester (a city full of the stresses of everyday life), the thrills of the railway journey (excitement, empowerment, and innovation) and the Loughborough destination (comparative arcadia, relaxation, and enjoyment). Cook's aim was to educate, and educate effectively.

A similar set of motives inspired the Reverend T A Leonard. The Congregational minister preached a sermon at Dockray Street Church in Colne in August 1891 in which he criticised the habit some people had of 'laking' about - playing - saying that "the devil wields no small influence over holiday times". Holidays should be taken sensibly, sacredly indeed. Leonard's view was "Speak to the earth and it will teach thee". The idea of education within holidays was present when Leonard went on to encourage a group of thirty men to organise a holiday in Ambleside in 1891, and Caernarfon the next.

By 1893, he was Secretary "of a scheme which embodies a new idea of summer holidays", inviting adult education classes and Pleasant Sunday Associations to join in visits to Ambleside and Keswick, walking by day and enjoying music and `lecturettes' in the evenings. The rambles were conducted by a University companion guide appointed by the National Home Reading Union (Speake, 1993). This was the beginning of the Co-operative Holidays Association, now the Countrywide Holidays Association and operating many holiday homes for its members.

Formal education out of doors is little covered in tourism books, yet it is one which by its variety and early encounter by students must underlie so much of their subsequent interest in travel. A very early example of this activity is that of the herbarizing organised by the Society of Apothecaries of London. This was the practical means by which apprentice apothecaries could be taught to recognise plants which would have medicinal values. The first one known took place in May of 1620, beginning at 5.OOam with a rendezvous at St Paul's in the City.

The day was spent out in the country, then relatively close by. Within a short while six excursions a year were being held. After a while a paid official known as the Demonstrator of Plants was employed to lead the excursions, and in 1673 the Chelsea Physic Garden was established as a permanent demonstration area. It has since become an important tourist attraction in its own right. Herbarizings continued up to 1824 when it was decided London was too big to allow for day excursions to open countryside, and the educational practice was abandoned. By then, many botanists had received their introduction to the subject through these events (Allen, 1976).

In 1732 The Society of Dilettante was formed from a group of men who had been on the Grand Tour. The Society helped to pioneer archaeological field study. Geology field teaching was in turn developed from 1804 by Robert Jameson of Edinburgh who took formal field classes as far away as the Western Isles. Geography field teaching in the UK got off to a relatively late start and in 1938 a survey of London schools showed that "hardly a half are able to conduct outdoor field work" (Dilke, 1965 p17). This was despite John Ruskin having said that "the country will become an outer and uncovered classroom, a Divine museum utilised by our teachers" (Reynolds, 1901). Excursions were the exception, rather than the rule.

One did occur in 1886, when Scott Keltie reported to the Royal Geographical society that the children of Gordon's Hospital School, Aberdeen, were "taken out into the country and in a simple, rough but effective, and to them, interesting and instructive way, are taught to draw maps of a small area for themselves" (Dilke, 1965). On the other hand, adult geographers made group excursions quite early. The Manchester Geographical Society went to inspect the new docks in Preston in the autumn of 1887 (Brown, 1971) for example. It should be remembered that individual adult travellers were being drawn towards industrial locations to see the changed landscapes presented from at least the 1780s onwards, as has been seen above. Field Societies, Scientific and Literary Societies and Geographical Societies continued through the nineteenth and twentieth centuries to make such excursions.

The practice widened out in the twentieth as manufacturers like Cadburys and Wedgwoods, anxious to promote their methods and products, opened their doors to all kinds of groups. Lever Brothers joined with the LMS railway company to promote tourism to their factory in Port Sunlight in 1926 (Cole and Durack, 1992). In the 1950s and 1960s both companies handled thousands of adult and school visitors. The present author recalls making visits to factories such as Lotus Shoes in Stone, British Rail Engineering in Crewe, a Co-op Dairy in Llangadog, the Velindre Tinplate Works and the Steel Company of Wales, Port Talbot. The steel and engineering companies used visits for general public relations purposes, the consumer goods makers used them to sell their wares. Even tiny manufacturers got involved, for example Joseph Dobson and Sons of Elland who from 1980 welcomed visitors in order to raise their profiles against their big competitors.

Indeed, Marling has recently shown how even that great icon of theme park tourism, Walt Disney, began with ideas for a "kiddies park" (Marling, 1997). Disney's new Burbank studio of 1939 was laid out on production-line principles. Having seen Snow White, people were asking to see how the animation was done. Disney thought that those who did visit found the whole process boring, and in any case there was none of the fairy tale magic on the production floor. So he began to plan a special area which would show both magic and motion picture production.

Early in the twentieth century it took people like James Fairgrieve, training geography teachers in the 1920s, to foster an interest in school excursions and holidays. He suggested children in east London could begin by finding out "information about the commodities that their fathers are handling". They could look at the doors of Fleet Street to see listed the newspapers of the British Empire as a starting point for discussing its geography. They would continue by making excursions to other places. "This is a benefit not only to the understanding of other lands but to the understanding of the homeland also. In a very real sense the homeland is measured by other lands: also, unless it is seen in its world setting, it is not really understood" (Fairgrieve, 1926). Factory visits were being added by progressive teachers at least from the late 1940s.

The nineteenth century was the great age of self-improving societies, often growing out of church or chapel groups who began to investigate interesting subjects. Others were specifically for self-help. The earliest - and still thriving with its private museum and lecture programme and visits - was the Spalding Gentlemen's' Society, founded in 1710. There were Mechanic's Institutes and worker's educational groups, and the subject societies for literary and scientific pursuits, from botany to geology and geography, many of which organised and ran their own excursions. In the United States similar self-help groups emerged in the diverse and often isolated settlements further west, while in the east urban groups sprang up, and the Chautauqua, already mentioned, had an important effect.

The original Chautauqua started as a summer vacation and training centre for Sunday School teachers at Chautauqua Lake, near to Lake Erie, in New York State. It developed as a place for discussion and debate on classical and current topics. Scholars, actors, speakers and exhibits were arranged, plays put on, great speeches re-made and debates staged (Colorado Chautauqua Association, 1997). Home-reading circles became part of the system, and for a time participants could study for a degree at a Chautauqua University.

The idea was imported to Britain largely through the work of J B Paton, who had been involved in setting up a University Extension in Nottingham. In 1887 Paton formed a small committee with John Percival, Headmaster of Rugby School, and from 1888 they organised Summer Meetings at Oxford with educational courses (Kelly, 1970). This line continued as the growth in the UK of adult education.

By the late nineteenth century the ideas of Frederic Le Play (Beaver, 1962) and then Patrick Geddes (Meller, 1990) had formed the basis for sociological field work with a strong geographical basis. Geddes' ideas has particularly interesting features in the context of the present paper. In Paris in 1878 he visited the International Exhibition and was enthusiastically inspired by the display of the reconstruction of Paris after the Franco-Prussian war of 1870. Returning to Edinburgh he became immersed in ideas of planning and improvement, one step in which was the purchase by him of the old Observatory at the lower end of the Castle Esplanade. It housed (and still does) a camera obscura which was used to project views of the city onto a white `projection table' for visitors to study.

Renamed the Outlook Tower and using whatever small funds and voluntary help that he could muster, Geddes began to create a kind of regional museum. He was also involved in teaching at the Edinburgh Summer Meetings or schools, linking the educational work with the displays in his Outlook Tower and excursions into Edinburgh to encourage city renewal.

Helen Meller, in Patrick Geddes: "Social Evolutionist and City Planner", shows how he absorbed ideas from the efforts of museums to collect and classify social knowledge (Meller, 1990). The Musee Sociale in Paris built on ideas which had been shown at the Paris Exhibitions of 1867, 1878 and 1889 about the study of people and their environs. The International Bibliographical Institute in Brussels was systematically collecting and classifying human knowledge in order to act as a centre of study. Geddes devised an idea for an `Index Museum' in his Outlook Tower with a kind of three-dimensional encyclopaedia of the world installed in it.

Geddes again went to an Exhibition in Paris, this time in 1900, organising a huge programme of lectures and tours in a Summer School there. "Eight hundred classes were held in just 120 days, and the average attendance at these was between 40 and 502" (Meller, 1990). And there at the Exhibition were pavilions and buildings from around the world. Geddes wanted to save them as a permanent `Index Museum', a centre of study of the world's cultures and societies. It failed to happen for reasons of cost and ownership.

Within the Paris Exhibition of 1900 the strands of education (Summer School), tourist attraction (the displays) and inspiration for progress (the ideas communicated by the displays and the School) came together. It did not become permanent: that would happen in museums and inter-activity centres in another age, perhaps more related to heritage than to visions of the future as Geddes wanted, but the principles, firmly based in educative forms of tourism, were all there.

A different - though related - reason was behind the origins of the Scout and Guide movement, which turned mere country visiting into an organised, structured, educationally-motivated activity. "Our business is not merely to keep up smart `show' troops, but to pass as many boys through our character factory as we possibly can: at the same time, the longer the grind that we can give them the better men they will be in the end" (Baden-Powell, 1908). Scouting was one of the occupations which, along with inspirational books like "Bevis: The Story of A Boy" (Jefferies,

1882) and "Swallows and Amazons" (Ransome, 1929) created the idea of adventure holidays which is at the heart of modem children's activity tourism. Jefferies educated his readers about the countryside: Baden-Powell trained his, through "Scouting For Boys" into adventurers who grew inwardly through their interaction with the rural environment.

As Michael Rosenthal shows, much of scout culture drew upon the works of the Anglo-American author, Ernest Thompson Seaton (Rosenthal, 1986). Between the 1880s and the 1900s Seton spread ideas of what he called Woodcraft' as a way for young American males to learn from, and be entertained by, life in the great outdoors.

He based his philosophy on the native North American culture and outlined a national movement based on features from his reading of native life, with a liberal dash of European chivalric ideas thrown in. Baden-Powell's movement adopted some of the ideas, but Seton's Woodcraft Indians continue still as a separate organisation. There was also an influence on the European Woodcraft Folk movement which grew amongst people who wanted a youth organisation which avoided what they saw as Baden-Powell's establishments and military leanings. Within one sector of tourism therefore it is possible to follow the development of a clear political/philosophical strand.

During the nineteenth century the growth and diversity of schooling allowed experimentation in terms of organisation and curriculum. Influenced by Rousseau's ideas about the importance of an individual's development some innovations were made which tried to relate teaching environments to the pupil's needs. In England, Cecil Reddie founded Abbotsholme School in 1889 as somewhere which could take a boy "to train him how to live". This meant daily, outdoor activities such as drill, sports, river bathing, running, carpentry and gardening.

Just after World War I Kurt Hahn co-founded Salem School in Germany with Prince Max von Baden, in which the development of character and selfdiscipline were foremost. Abbotsholme had had an influence. With the arrival of Nazism Kurt Hahn was forced to leave, and he moved to Britain_ In late 1933 he opened Gordonstoun School in Scotland, with a disciplinarian programme which included ideas of service to the nearby community. From 1935 onwards boys were enrolled as HM Coastguards, and they later operated a small fire brigade. The `Moray Badge' scheme was devised with tests in athletics, expeditions, and life-saving, partly in response to a national debate about the poor quality of fitness in young people (Hahn, 1957). It is interesting to note the similarities to matching fears expressed at the turn of the century about the health and character of boys which helped lead to the Boy Scouts.

Out of the Badge scheme came three experimental; residential summer schools in Invemess-shire and Morayshire. Their success led in turn to the formation of the Outward Bound schools, this time in Wales, at Aberdovey, to which Gordonstoun had been evacuated on the outbreak of war. From 1941 an Outward Bound Sea School commenced operation, offering courses to young men from industry, not only in maritime activities, but also 30-mile mountain country expeditions (Hahn, 1957). The Outward Bound movement has also grown and expanded its activities to a number of British and European centres.

In Germany the idea of the school excursion had gained ground rapidly from 1907 and the formation of the 'wandervogel' at Jena in January that year. Its aims were "to promote rambles and excursions of German boys in their own and other neighbourhoods, and thus to awaken in them a taste for the beauties of nature, and to give them opportunities of learning to know their German homeland and its people at first hand" (Thomson and Haehnel, 1909). Local associations were set up and older children encouraged to qualify as guides. Books and maps were bought and could be hired out to non-members. Travel and overnight accommodation were to be simple - fourth-class rail and country barns.

Earlier still, the Eberfeld 'Realgymnasium' was one of several schools which held indoor lessons until noon and then gymnastics or excursions. On six afternoons in the summer term the whole four hundred children at Eberfeld would march out of town behind a band, the older children going the furthest, and teachers instructing the pupils along the way. Games would round off the excursion, for which six hours was allowed. The government extended the Whit holiday to allow higher classes make longer journeys to places like the Westerwald, Taunus and Eiffel districts. Up to twenty boys and their masters might make a fortnight's visit to somewhere like Italy. The days started early and consisted of long walks followed by evening recreation ("beer and songs") and summaries by the boys of what they had done - often given in foreign languages. The pupils paid themselves in advance, with poorer boys charged less, but "for poor masters no funds were provided" (Bahre, 1901). It is noteworthy that German interest in exploring environments seems to have underpinned the country's ideas in gestalt psychology, to which reference will be made later.

Another organisation began in Germany in the same year, 1907, that Baden-Powell was holding his first scout camp on Brownsea Island in Poole Harbour. A teacher, Richard Schirmann, opened his school to a group of children from slum areas, so that they could enjoy a countryside holiday. Two years later Altena Town Council and a local businessman gave money to turn Burg Altena into a hostel. It was the start of the 'wandervogel' movement, anti-militarist, anti-machinery, pro-country life. Britain set up its first hostel in 1930 though a water-supply problem forced it to close soon afterwards. The YHA dates from that year, and the next year saw no fewer than twenty hostels open

(Coburn, 1950). Country life, exploration and adventure were the aims of all their visitors.

In Britain all of these strands became woven together after 1945 and new ones were added. The Field Studies Council in Britain opened its first centre in Suffolk in 1946, and the first local authority centre, White Hall near Buxton, opened in 1950 (Parker and Meldrum, 1973). National Parks, open air museums, commercially-run adventure centres, stately homes and historic houses, castles and wartime defences, zoos and sea-life centres, gardens and country parks, heritage centres and inter-active science centres, factory tours and craft demonstration units made their appearances on ever larger scales. Were these just part of a heritage industry making new money, or an extension of the very long growth of educational tourism? School visits, especially when linked to the National Curriculum, can provide the bread-and-butter visitor income that they need to survive.

This account of some of the educational aspects of tourism is not complete, nor could it be within the confines of a discussion paper. Nor does it attempt to discuss in detail who benefited from each, nor just how much benefit there was, nor how prejudiced or enlightened any of it might have been. What is important here is the acknowledgement of the frequent close liaison that there has always been in tourism with education. It is fair, and appropriate, to say that all forms of information and opinion, whether expressed between individuals, through the mass media, or in education, are subject to limitations on access, quality and objectivity. The point is that tourism is just as good, or just as bad, as they are. But it has, like them, a potential for being beneficial.

CHAPTER–3

INTERNATIONAL EDUCATION

International education can mean many different things and its definition is debated. Some have defined two general meanings to the concept of international education in regard to students. The first refers to education that transcends national borders through the exchange of people, as in study abroad and student exchange program. The second, explored in depth here, is a comprehensive approach to education that intentionally prepares students to be active and engaged participants in an interconnected world.

The International Baccalaureate defines the term according to criteria such as the development of citizens of the world in accordance to culture, language, and social cohesion, building a sense of identity and cultural awareness, encrypting recognition and development of universal human values, encourage discovery and enjoyment of learning, equip students with collectivist or individualistic skills and knowledge that can be applied broadly, encourage global thinking when responding to local situations,encourage diversity and flexibility in teaching pedagogies and supply appropriate forms of assessment and international benchmarking.

Understanding of a broad array of phenomena is enhanced and deepened through examination of the cultures, languages, environmental situations, governments, political relations, religions, geography, and history of the world. While definitions vary in the precise language used, international education is generally taken to include:

- Knowledge of other world regions & cultures;
- Familiarity with international and global issues;
- Skills in working effectively in global or cross-cultural environments, and using information from different sources around the world;
- Ability to communicate in multiple languages; and
- Dispositions towards respect and concern for other cultures and peoples.

MILLENNIUM DEVELOPMENT GOALS

International education is also a major part of international development. Professionals and students wishing to be a part of international education development are able to learn through organizations and university and college programs. Organizations around the world use education as a means to development. The United Nations Millennium Development Goals include to education specific goals:

- Achieve universal primary education in all countries by 2015
- Eliminate gender disparity in primary and secondary education by 2015

Other mentions of education in regard to international development: Education For All (EFA): An international strategy to operazionalize the Dakar Framework for Action; The World Education Forum (Dakar 2000) agreed to reach 6 goals by 2015:

- expand early childhood care and education
- improve access to complete, free schooling of good quality for all primary school-age children

- greatly increase learning opportunities for youth and adults
- improve adult literacy rates by 50%
- eliminate gender disparities in schooling
- improve all aspects of education quality.

Dakar Framework for Action

UN Decade of Education for Sustainable Development (2005-2014) -highlight the central role of education in the pursuit of sustainable development.

International education both as a field of study focusing on study abroad and preparing students for international occupations as well as an active part of international development is taught in many colleges and universities around the world.

International Education Week

International Education Week is held in the United States by the U.S. Department of State and U.S. Department of Education during the week before Thanksgiving; the week is November 15-19 in 2010, November 14-18 in 2011, and November 12-16 in 2012. The benefits of this event are to provide an opportunity to celebrate the benefits of International Education and global exchange.

This joint initiative are efforts to promote programs that prepare Americans for a global milieu and attract future leaders from abroad to study, learn and exchange experiences in the U.S. This shows how International education is not just about physically crossing borders, but is also about thinking globally in local situations.

Challenges Facing International Education

International education has a somewhat unusual position in higher education. While recognized as an important sphere of activity, it tends to be handled by administrative offices at the top of departments of languages and literature and international affairs. The scholars involved in international education usually have their primary involvement in other teaching and research. This leads to four distinctive characteristics particular to the field of international education:

1. There is little consensus concerning the guiding theme of the field as well as its scope. Should the field stress internationalization, transnationalization, or globalization?
2. International education is not a prominent feature of the contemporary higher education experience. Using enrollment in foreign languages as an indicator, 16 percent of all U.S. college students were enrolled in foreign languages in the peak period of the 1960s; the proportion is currently down to 8 percent.
3. There is imbalance in regional coverage. The regions and languages covered at a particular institution are a function of idiosyncratic patterns of faculty recruitment. Nationally, there is reasonable coverage of Western Europe and Latin America and most European languages compared to limited coverage of Africa and the Middle East. For students enrolled in foreign languages, Spanish is the most popular followed by the other major languages of Western Europe; 6 percent enroll in Asian languages. Languages of the Middle East make up only 2 percent (1.3 being Hebrew and .5 percent Arabic). The languages of Africa constitute only 0.15 percent of enrollments.
4. Because international education is not a primary concern of most scholars in the field, research is somewhat sporadic, non-cumulative, and tends to be carried out by national organizations as part of

advocacy projects (e.g. Lambert, 1989; Brecht and Rivers, 2000). The most recent example is the American Council of Education's (ACE's) Internationalization of Higher Education: A Status Report.

STUDY ABROAD IN THE UNITED STATES

Studying abroad is the act of a student pursuing educational opportunities in a country other than one's own. This can include primary, secondary and post-secondary students. In the United States, 260,327 students studied abroad for academic credit in 2008-2009, which represented a modest decline of 0.8% from the previous year's record high of 262,214, according to the most recent "Open Doors Report on International Education Exchange" report. The number of students studying abroad still represents only about 1% of all students enrolled at institutions of higher education in the United States.

While the majority of foreign students who study in the United States are pursuing a full degree, most outgoing U.S. students study abroad for one or two academic terms. The majority of US students now choose short-term study abroad programs according to the most recent Institute of International Education Open Doors Report. In the 2008-09 academic year, the five countries US students chose to study abroad in most were the United Kingdom, Italy, Spain, France, and China.

The total number of US students studying abroad during 2008-09 was 260,327, compared to 262,416 the previous year, a modest decline of 0.8%. The Open Doors report is published annually by the Institute of International Education with funding from the U.S. Department of State's Bureau of Educational and Cultural Affairs. However, the report found that there were notable increases in the number of U.S. students going to study in less traditional destinations. Fifteen of the top 25 destinations were outside of Western

Europe and nineteen were countries where English is not a primary language.

History

The University of Delaware is typically credited with creating the first study abroad program designed for U.S. undergraduate students in the 1920s. Professor Raymond W. Kirkbride, a French professor and World War I veteran, won support from university president Walter S. Hullihen to send students to France to study during their junior year. UD initially refused to fund Kirkbride's travels, and he and Hullihen appealed to prominent public and private figures for support including then-Secretary of Commerce Herbert Hoover and businessman Pierre S. du Pont.

Kirkbride set sail for on July 7, 1923 with eight students for six weeks of intensive language courses in Nancy, France before moving on to Paris to study at The Sorbonne. The Delaware Foreign Study Plan, which came to be known as the Junior Year Abroad (JYA), was considered a success and was replicated by other U.S. institutions, such as Smith College. In 1948, the Delaware Foreign Study Plan was discontinued due to post-war conditions in Europe and shifting priorities under a new university president. It has since been re-instated in the form of their current study abroad program.

Trends

Despite flat overall study abroad numbers, there were notable increases in the numbers of U.S. students going to some of the less traditional destinations for study abroad in 2008/09. Double digit increases to host countries among the top 25 destinations include Argentina, Chile, Denmark, the Netherlands, Peru, South Africa and South Korea. Double-digit decreases among the top 25 host countries include Mexico (which experienced H1N1 virus outbreak that year), Austria and India.

The following table represents the top 25 study abroad destinations for U.S. students seeking academic credit in 2007/08 and 2008/09, according to the Institute of International Education.

Rank	Destination	2007/08	2008/09	2008/09 % of Total	% Change
	World Total	262,416	260,327	100.0	-0.8
1	United Kingdom	33,333	31,342	12.0	-6.0
2	Italy	30,670	27,362	10.5	-10.8
3	Spain	25,212	24,169	9.3	-4.1
4	France	17,336	16,910	6.5	-2.5
5	China	13,165	13,674	5.3	3.9
6	Australia	11,042	11,140	4.3	0.9
7	Germany	8,253	8,330	3.2	0.9
8	Mexico	9,928	7,320	2.8	-26.3
9	Ireland	6,881	6,858	2.6	-0.3
10	Costa Rica	6,096	6,363	2.4	4.4
11	Japan	5,710	5,784	2.2	1.3
12	Argentina	4,109	4,705	1.8	14.5
13	South Africa	3,700	4,160	1.6	12.4
14	Czech Republic	3,417	3,664	1.4	7.2
15	Greece	3,847	3,616	1.4	-6.0
16	Chile	2,739	3,503	1.3	27.9
17	Ecuador	2,814	2,859	1.1	1.6
18	Austria	3,356	2,836	1.1	-15.5
19	Brazil	2,723	2,777	1.1	2.0
20	New Zealand	2,629	2,769	1.1	5.3
21	India	3,146	2,690	1.0	-14.5
22	Netherlands	2,038	2,318	0.9	13.7
23	Denmark	1,855	2,244	0.9	21.0
24	Peru	1,638	2,163	0.8	32.1
25	South Korea	1,597	2,062	0.8	29.1

Types of Programs

Despite the slight decline in U.S. students studying abroad for credit in 2008-2009, study abroad is likely to continue to grow. The number of outgoing U.S. students pursuing overseas study has increased over fivefold since the late 1980s, from less than 50,000 students to more than 260,000 in 2008-09. Behind the numbers, though, has been the proliferation in the type study abroad programs. According to Lilli Engel of the American University Center of Provence, there are fundamental differences in the academic and cultural experience offered by study abroad programs today that suggest the need to create a level-based classification system for program types.

In an influential Frontiers: The Interdisciplinary Journal of Study Abroad article, she compares "a one-month summer term, requiring little or no host language proficiency, with subject-matter classes in English, collective housing and American roommates" with "a full-year program for students of advanced linguistic proficiency housed individually in a host family and directly enrolled in local university courses or engaged in a professional internship or service-learning project."

Yet, within international education a universally-accepted method of classifying study abroad programs has proven elusive. U.S. students can choose from a wide range of study abroad opportunities differentiated by program sponsor, curriculum, cost, program model, language and degree of integration, to name a few. While study abroad in the U.S. is by no means uniform, study abroad programs can reasonably be grouped according to (a) duration, (b) program model (c) program sponsor.

Four Basic Program Models

Four basic models have been identified to refer to a study abroad program's structure. They consist of (a) Island, (b) Integrated, (c) Hybrid, and (d) Field-study programs.

- Island - Students participating in island programs study alongside other American students in a study center. Island programs are typically sponsored U.S. universities and/or third-party providers, who develop a curriculum specifically with American students in mind.
- Integrated Students who participate on an integrated program enroll directly in courses alongside local students at a host university. Program sponsors may provide additional services such as assistance with course registration and language tutoring.
- Hybrid - Hybrid programs include elements of both island and integrated program. Typically students take a selection of their coursework at a host university and the remainder at a study center. Hybrid programs are common in countries where the primary language of instruction is not English, such as China and Morocco.
- Field-based - Field-based study abroad programs for academic credit are structured much more liberally than traditional island, integrated or hybrid programs. Generally these programs involve a thematic focus, field study training and finally an independent study project. SIT Study Abroad programs are for the most part field-based.

Program Sponsor

Programs can also be grouped and classified by identifying a program's sponsor. Sponsors are the institutions and/or circumstances that led to a program's creation, as well as what the goal of a program is. The main study abroad program sponsors are (a) host university (direct exchange and direct enroll), (c) U.S. college or university (study centers and international branch campuses), and (c) study abroad organizations known as third-party providers.

Host University Sponsor: direct exchange and direct enroll.

Many U.S. institutions have long-standing direct exchange partnerships with foreign institutions that allow their students to enroll in classes as a visiting student while still paying standard tuition at their home university. Direct exchanges are facilitated by agreements governing academic credit transfer and financial aid between the home university and host university.

While individual agreements may vary, direct exchange typically involves a 1:1 where the number of inbound exchange must be equivalent to the number of outgoing study abroad students. Typically, students enroll in standard courses at the host institution and are fully integrated with host country students and are responsible for their own housing, airport transfer, etc. Programs are administered on-site by the host university, with pre-departure advising and assistance from a U.S. university study abroad office.

Like direct exchange, direct enrollment programs are generally geared toward the more independent student, as participants enroll in courses directly alongside local students. Students are responsible for their housing and coordinating other logistics. Unlike direct exchanges, direct enrollment does not necessarily require an agreement between the U.S. institution and the foreign university. As such, credit transfer is not automatic and participants pay tuition and fees directly to the host university.

Sponsored by U.S. College and Universities: study centers and international branch campuses.

Some of the most popular study abroad programs include those sponsored by a student's home institution, by another U.S. college or university, or by a consortium of U.S. colleges or universities. These programs are designed to allow students to study in a foreign environment while remaining within a U.S. academic framework. Credit transfer is arranged by the sponsoring and programs typically align with traditional U.S. academic calendars.

The U.S. sponsor institution will typically assist with housing arrangements, and may arrange cultural activities and excursions for participating students. Study center are known as "island programs" because create separate classes and spaces for U.S. and foreign students. Participants may take classes at a study center or international branch campus run by the U.S. college or university sponsor. The curriculum of study centers are specifically designed for study abroad students.

For example, students at Texas Tech University's Seville, Spain program study with TTU faculty, take TTU courses with other TTU students and earn TTU credit. International branch campuses, however, are distinct in that U.S. study abroad students enroll in classes alongside full degree-seeking students. As an example, Florida State University Panama Canal Branch offers a broad curriculum and the majority of its students are Panamanian or are from other countries in Latin America, Notably Colombia and Costa Rica. Today, U.S. colleges and universities operate at least 80 international branch campuses worldwide.

Sponsored by third-party Providers

Third-party providers are private companies and organizations that sponsor study abroad programs. Both for-profit and non-profit third-party providers assist program participants with logistics like course registration and housing arrangements. While models differ, academic and social guidance is generally included throughout the duration of a program, as are built-in excursions and community service opportunities.

Third-party providers of all stripes pursue relationships with U.S. universities in the form of affiliation agreements or membership consortia agreements. There are many third-party providers in operation in the United States. Program models vary; please find a partial list below:

- o American Institute For Foreign Study (AIFS), based in Stamford, Connecticut
- o Academic Programs International (API), based in Austin, Texas
- o Academic Studies Abroad (ASA), based in Roslindale, Massachusetts
- o Arcadia University Center for Education Abroad, based in Glenside, Pennsylvania
- o Athena Study Abroad, based in Columbus, Ohio
- o Boston University International Programs, based in Boston, Massachusetts
- o CEA Global Education, based in Tempe, Arizona
- o CEPA Europe, based in Ingersheim, Germany
- o CET Academic Programs, based in Washington, DC
- o Council on International Education and Exchange (CIEE), based in Portland, Maine
- o Danish Institute for Study Abroad, affiliated with the University of Copenhagen.
- o Global Links Learning Abroad, based in Westminster, Colorado
- o Institute for the International Education of Students (IES), based in Chicago, Illinois
- o Institute for Study Abroad (IFSA), affiliated with Butler University in Indianapolis, Indiana
- o interstudy, based in Medford, Massachusetts
- o International Studies Abroad (ISA), based in Austin, Texas
- o International Student Exchange Programs (ISEP), based in Washington, DC

- o School for International Training (SIT Study Abroad), based in Brattleboro, Vermont
- o Study Abroad Italy (SAI), based in Sebastopol, California
- o The Education Abroad Network (TEAN), based in South Bend, Indiana
- o University Studies Abroad Consortium (USAC), based in Reno, Nevada

Funding Study Abroad

Costs for a study abroad program include, but are not limited to tuition and fees, room and board, medical insurance, passport and visa fees and transportation costs. While U.S. universities vary in terms of policies related to financing study abroad, financial aid for U.S. students who wish to study abroad may include a combination of scholarships, grants from the home university, government student loans, and private student loans.

An amendments made in 1992 to the Higher Education Act of 1965, TITLE VI, SEC. 601-604 in the U.S. ruled that students can receive financial aid for study abroad if they are enrolled in a program that is approved by their home institution and would be eligible to receive government funding without regard to whether the study abroad program is required as a part of the student's degree.

Federal Grants

- The Pell Grant - The Pell Grant is a need-based grant. To qualify, you must be a full-time undergraduate student with an Expected Family Contribution (EFC) below the limit determined each year
- The Federal Supplemental Education Opportunities Grant - This need-based grant is awarded to those students demonstrating the greatest financial need.

Students typically must qualify for the federal Pell Grant to receive an SEOG Grant

Federal Loans

- Federal Stafford Loan - The Stafford Loan is in your name and is available to all students, regardless of financial need. If the loan is subsidized, the government will pay the interest while you are in school. If the loan is unsubsidized, you have the option of capitalizing the interest or of paying the interest quarterly during the in-school period. Payment of the principle itself (for both subsidized and unsubsidized loans) does not begin until six months after graduation, provided you remain enrolled on at least a half-time (six credits) basis.
- Federal Perkins Loan - The Perkins Loan is a low-interest loan (5 percent) awarded to those students demonstrating the greatest financial need.
- Parent PLUS Loans for Undergraduate Students - Parents may borrow up to the full cost of a student's education, less the amount of any other financial aid received. There is a minimal credit check required for the PLUS loan, so a good credit history is required.

Federal Scholarships

- David L. Boren Undergraduate Scholarships for Study Abroad - The National Security Education Program (NSEP) provides scholarships to undergraduate students who wish to study languages and cultures considered to be important to U.S. national security. Students are not eligible to receive the Boren scholarship if they are studying in Australia, Austria, Belgium, Canada, Denmark, Finland, France, Germany, Greece, Iceland, Ireland, Italy, Luxembourg, the Netherlands, New Zealand,

Norway, Portugal, Spain, Sweden, Switzerland, or the United Kingdom.

- Benjamin A. Gilman International Scholarship - If you receive a federal Pell Grant, you are eligible to apply for a Gilman Scholarship.

Criticism

In mid-2007, New York's attorney general opened an inquiry into the relationships between universities and providers of study abroad. According to the lawyer, Benjamin Lawsky, deputy counselor in the office of Attorney General Andrew M. Cuomo, the inquiry was to focus on whether cash incentives and other perks that study abroad providers give universities influence their decisions about where students may study. Critics contend that the practices, rarely disclosed and largely unknown, limit study abroad options and drive up the price that is ultimately passed onto students. The investigation follows disclosures in The New York Times that providers of study abroad are offering colleges rebates, free and subsidized travel, unpaid seats on advisory boards, help with back-office services and marketing stipends. In some cases, perks are tied to the number of students universities send to a given provider's program. When asked, Lawsky said that the inquiry grew out of his office's inquiries into similar practices in the student loan industry.

As part of the investigation, Cuomo's office issued subpoenas for five of the major study abroad providers in August 2007. The first batch of providers were the Institute for Study Abroad at Butler University, the American Institute for Foreign Study, the Institute for the International Education of Students; the Center for Education Abroad at Arcadia University, and the Danish Institute for Study Abroad. Six months later, he issued subpoenas or requests for documents top 15 colleges in and out of New York State. In light of the unprecedented attention on the industry,

NAFSA: Association of International Educators drafted a report in early 2008 calling on U.S. university study abroad offices to be more open in their decision making and to demonstrate that their policies directly benefit students.

Also in response to Cuomo's investigation, the Forum on Education Abroad released a code of ethics in March 2008 that sought to be a "compass" for U.S. universities, study abroad providers and foreign host institutions. Unlike the NAFSA report, the forum document offers a broad set of ethical principles and detailed guidance. It recommends, amongst other things, that U.S. institutions have specific procedures for reporting payments, like honoraria and consulting fees, for work done on behalf of providers; that agreements and criteria for selecting study abroad programs be disclosed fully; and that the goals and parameters for visits by campus officials to overseas program sites be clearly established in advance of the trips. The forum is a consortium of American and overseas colleges and outside providers founded in 2001 to create standards of good practices for education abroad.

STUDENT EXCHANGE PROGRAM

A student exchange program generally could be defined as a program where students from secondary school or university choose to study abroad in partner institutions. The terms 'student exchange' and 'study abroad' are often used interchangeably, however study abroad usually involves the student study full time and not in partnered institution like student going for exchange where they will be studying in the partner university of their home institution.

But in some countries, an exchange student is also considered a study abroad student because they are studying in different country than their own. Student exchange program does not necessarily require the student going out of the country but it could also be an exchange program within the continent and its territory which is the National student exchange program (NSE).

The term "exchanges" means that partnered institution exchange their student but not necessarily the students have to find a counterpart from the other institution to exchange with. No tradeoff is actually required. Two types of student exchange program are international and national student exchange program. A student exchange programs could be joined either by the secondary school or university student excluding National Student Exchange where it is design primarily for university student studying in American continent and its territory.

An exchange student could live with a host family or in a designated place including hostels, affordable apartment/ house or student lodge. The cost for each program differs according to countries and institution. The participants could either apply/receive scholarship, self-funded or apply/ receive loan.

Student exchanges became popular after World War II, and have the aim of helping to increase the participants' understanding and tolerance of other cultures, as well as improving their language skills and broadening their social horizons.An exchange student typically stays in the host country for a relatively short period of time, often 6 to 10 months, in contrast to international students or those on study abroad programs which can last for several years.

Some students on exchange programs can receive academic credit from the country they study in.

Objectives

- To enhance the educational experience of student
- To strengthen the networking between students and Universities
- Broaden personal and educational perspectives

- Explore, appreciate and understand different cultures
- To enhance the ability of the student in second language learning
- To eliminate fear and prejudice among nations
- Enable student to experience international education

TYPES OF EXCHANGE PROGRAMS

National Exchange Programs

National Student Exchange (NSE) is a not-for-profit education consortium, provides affordable and practical opportunities for students enrolled at member campuses to study and live in a new location. More than 94,000 students have participated in this program since it was founded in 1968. NSE is designed for students who are looking for chances to study in different state rather than country.

This may be due to lack of interest in going overseas, or doesn't have the chance to go or just wanting to gain experience on different culture and education but closer to home. NSE is only available in the American continent and its territories (United States, Canada, Guam, Puerto Rico, and the U.S. Virgin Islands) where universities and colleges that are members of NSE will receive and send student for exchange. Students are not allowed to go for an exchange to non NSE members.

To date, there are nearly 200 universities and colleges that have registered as NSE members. Application process, placement and pre-departure process will be coordinated fully by the home NSE coordinator. Student could choose whether to pay the tuition fees to home campus or host campus. Student may only participate in the exchange for a cumulative total of time not to exceed one calendar year, defined as an academic year and a summer session.

INTERNATIONAL EXCHANGE PROGRAMS

Short-term Exchange

Short term exchange program is also known as summer/ intensive or cultural exchange program that focus on homestays, language skills, community service or cultural activities. Short term exchange program doesn't require student to find counterpart from other country to exchange with. It is more on the exchange of culture between the student and host countries. High school and universities student could apply for the program from various government or non-governmental organization that organize the programs.

This program could last from one week to three month and doesn't require the student to study in any particular school or institution. The students are exposed to an intensive program that increases their understanding of other culture, community and languages. Here are some examples of short term student exchange program and organization:

- AFS (American Field Service) Intercultural Program
- Lions International Youth Exchange Program
- Southern Cross Cultural exchange
- EATOF (East Asia Inter-Regional Tourism Forum)   Summer Youth Camp
- AYUSA Global Youth Exchange Summer Study Abroad Program
- Rotary International
- List of Summer Programs by Country

Long-term Exchange

A long term exchange is considered an exchange which is designed to last six to ten months or up to one full year. Participants are to attend high school in their host countries, through a student visa. Typically, non-USA students coming to the USA are issued J-1 Cultural Exchange Visas though some programs may use the F-1 Foreign Student Visa. Students are expected to integrate themselves into the host family, living as a natural child would, immersing themselves in the local community and surroundings, and upon their return to their home country are expected to incorporate this knowledge into their daily lives, as well as give a presentation on their experience to their sponsors. This is a hallmark of the AFS and Rotary programs.

Many exchange programs expect students to be able converse in the language of the new host country, at least on a basic level. Some programs require students to pass a standardized test for English language comprehension, for example, prior to being accepted into a program taking them to the United States. Others do not examine basic language communication ability. Most exchange students become fluent in the language of the host country in which they are a new student within a few months. Some exchange programs, such as the Congress-Bundestag Youth Exchange are government-funded programs.

Most programs do not require an actual exchange of individual students between countries. Instead the majority of exchange students are those coming into the U.S., without any American leaving the U.S. The exchange consists of the foreign student and the host parents or host family sharing culture and comparing daily life and habits while building a natural friendship that will endure beyond the actual exchange year. The focus is on improving international relations and cultural understanding.There has been some concern about the safety of foreign exchange students due to lack of regulation of the host families and legal differences between the exchanging countries.

Application Process

Long term (10 to 12 month) exchange applications and interviews generally take place 10 months in advance of departure, but sometimes as little as four months. Ages requirements are between 15 and 18.5, older or younger cannot be classified as a foreign exchange student. Some programs allow students older than 18 years of age in a specialized work-study program. DM Discoveries in particular has work abroad programs for students older than 18 years of age and out of high school.

Some programs first require a preliminary application with fees, then schedule interviews and request a longer application. Other programs request a full application from the beginning and then schedule interviews to more completely expand on the application information. High school scholarship programs often require a set GPA of around 3.0 or higher. These programs choose their students via application and personal interview, selecting the candidates most likely to complete the program and serve as the best ambassadors to the foreign nation.

Students in some programs are expected to go to any location where the organization places them, such as Rotary, and students are encouraged not to have strict expectations of their host country. Such open attitudes often make for a more enjoyable exchange. Students do make a country choice, but may live at any spot within that country.

Most programs expect the prospective exchange student to demonstrate some ability to speak the language of the country they choose. However, requirements of ability to communicate vary: the organization in the home country of the student (the country to which the student has applied) often makes this decision. The home country organization will then have a partner organization in the country of the student's choice.

Students accepted for the program may or may not be screened by the organization in their home country. Partner organizations in the destination country each have differing levels of screening they require students to pass through before being accepted into their program. For example, students coming to the U.S. may be required by a U.S. partner organization to submit as little as the recommendation by the organization in their home country (who also collects a fee from the student) or the U.S. partner may require student applicants to submit detailed application materials such as previous school report cards, and letters from their school teachers and administrators in addition to the original standardized English fluency exam papers. The U.S. agency may then accept or decline the applicant.

Some U.S. organizations also have Rules of Participation requirements. Almost all U.S. organizations cannot allow an exchange student to drive an automobile, for example, due to liability costs that would cause program costs and thus fees to be out of reach for most students. Some organizations require written contract standards for personal behavior and grades, while others may be less rigorous.

Frequently foreign parents will choose a program based on the lowest cost, which can result in a student participating in a program without a supervisor for the student living close enough to check on the student's well-being frequently. Programs provided by agencies that provide compensation for Representatives are more likely to retain local Representatives to assist and guide the student and remain closely aware of the student's well-being. Thus a program that pays its Representatives is more likely to have Representatives available locally as well as activities for the students.

Costs

Programs vary depending upon program length, country, content and other factors. Most program costs include insurance and other risk management components, especially health insurance. Students going on university exchange could pay tuition fees on home campus or host campus, but most of the time it is paid to home campus. Long term exchange program for university student often comes with Scholarship that covers most of the expenses including flight ticket, accommodation and daily necessities. Secondary school exchange program often provided with scholarship but most of the time it is self-funded by their parents.

ACCOMMODATION

Host Family

A host family is a volunteered family that welcomes student from different place or countries to stay with them during the exchange program period. This is particularly arranged for secondary school student and cultural exchange programs. The family often doesn't receive any payment for hosting but the students are responsible for their own financial spending this include school fees, uniform, text books, internet and phone calls.

A host family could come in many different forms including retired couples, single parents with or without children, couples with primary school children, couples with teenagers and a family pet and others. Host families have the responsibility to at least provide a room, meals, and a stable family environment for the student.

Of course there is the natural possibility that problems may arise while living with any host family. In this case, most exchange programs allow for a switch of families. In each family, it is required to have one parent who is at least 25 years of age. The families that have been selected are well prepared to experience new culture and give a new cultural experience to the student. A student could live with more than one family in an exchange program to expand their knowledge and experience new culture.

Housing

University student going on exchange program could choose either to live on campus or off campus. Living on campus will require them to compete with other local students for a place. Living off campus is a popular choice among student going for exchange because they would like to be independent and learn new culture on their own. Universities that host student exchange program do have special assistance for the student to seek accommodation.

Universities in Asia particularly, have on-campus housing for the international student that is on exchange or studying full time. So, they don't have to seek other accommodation outside the universities. Living in shared house, student lodge or apartment/hostels often come with 6 or more month contract depending on the length of stay in a particular institution or countries. Personal budget and lifestyle preference should also be taken into consideration before making an arrangement for accommodation.

Students are advice to search for accommodation as soon as they receive their acceptance letter and student visa. Student should also have a backup plan if the house they are interested in is unavailable. Temporary accommodation such as backpacker motels or hotel is available for renting until student are able to find a permanent place to stay. Student could also arrange for a homestay if it is available in that particular country. Homestay is similar to Host Family but student have to pay them for the daily necessity that the family will provide for them this include room, food and others.

BENEFITS

1. Educational

- International learning and knowledge propels students towards acceptance and understanding of an array of different cultural and community perspectives.

- Language acquisition is achieved through practical immersion.
- Increase awareness and adoption of alternative, multi-faceted approaches to learning.
- Acquire analytical and problem solving skills.
- Enhanced interest in global issues as well as broadening general knowledge.

2. Personal

- Self-development and awareness leading to enhanced self-confidence and self-esteem. This is often the most noticeable change in returned exchange students.
- Enhance maturity and social poise; fuelled by the necessity to confront challenges outside a familiar support network and comfort zone.
- The integration into another family as well as the development of life-long friendships could foster an appreciation of home and family.
- A tremendous sense of accomplishment upon completion encourages students to develop independent opinions, make informed decisions and strive to attain fresh goals.

3. Long-term

- Students who go on to tertiary studies find themselves more comfortable in 'foreign' environments.
- Prospective employers in almost every field look favourably upon experience gained while living overseas and knowledge obtained of another language and culture.

- Increased pressure to communicate and relate to others develops an awareness of group dynamics and personal sensitivity towards others
- Successful program completion represents an excellent measure of personal flexibility, encompassing an ability to reach compromise, focus and succeed through challenging times.

INTERNATIONAL YOUTH MEETINGS

Very often the term "youth exchange" (often associated with student exchanges) is used also for international youth meetings. This is true in Europe, for example, for the "Youth in Action Programme" of the EU. Such activities are not student's exchanges per se, but meeting where groups of young people (age 15-30) form different countries live together, engage in activities planned and implemented by them, and learn about each others culture while discussing of different topics of social interest.

In Europe the amount of such project is relatively high; the budget for this programme, which also includes other types of projects such as volunteering abroad, training courses and youth initiatives, for 6 years (2006-2013) is of almost 1 billion Euros. It involves all the EU countries as well as EuroMediterranean countries, Balkan area and East Europe and Caucasus, even if a smaller budget is reserved for them.

CHAPTER–4

ROLE OF TRAVEL AGENT

A travel agent plays a vital role in promoting educational tourism. Travel agents plan, organize, and conduct long distance cruises, tours and expeditions for individuals or groups. The responsibility of the travel agent is to assist travelers with the constantly changing airfares and schedules, thousands of available vacation packages, and a vast amount of travel information on the internet.

Tourism and the entities that make up this multibillion-dollar industry are somewhat familiar to all of us through firsthand contact. Though we may not have been able to experience all parts of the tourism industry, we do have distinct impressions and recollections of the ones we have.

For example, those who have recently taken a cruise understand that, along with a boat ride, one enjoys fine dining and entertainment, a variety of recreational activities, shopping, socializing, and sightseeing. We quickly come to understand that cruising is not just a boat ride, but also an adventure in the "rest and relaxation" industry. In the past, cruising was only for older people and their parents, but now it is for everyone.

The cruise business is only a small segment of the tourism industry. Other vital components in the tourism industry include airlines, hotels, rental cars, rail lines, motor-coaches, tour operators, travel agents, limousines, charter operators, and convention bureaus.

Each of these entities realizes that it is selling more than what meets the eye. They all hope to have a positive impact on our senses so we will use them again and again.

HAVING A POSITIVE EXPERIENCE

For me, having a positive experience each time I travel doesn't always happen. This may be due to the fact that I do most of my traveling while on business trips, and, thus, have business on my mind.

To sort out the many travel options, tourists and business people often turn to travel agents, who assess their needs and help them make the best possible travel arrangements. Also, many major cruise ships, resorts, and specialty travel groups use travel agents to promote travel packages to millions of people every year.

In general, travel agents give advice on destinations and make arrangements for transportation, hotel accommodations, car rentals, tours, and recreation. They also may advise on weather conditions, restaurants, tourist attractions, and recreation. For international travel, agents also provide information on customs regulations, required papers (passports, visas, and certificates of vaccination), and currency exchange rates.

Travel agents consult a variety of published and computer-based sources for information on departure and arrival times, fares, and hotel ratings and accommodations. They may visit hotels, resorts, and restaurants to evaluate their comfort, cleanliness, and the quality of food and service so that they can base recommendations on their own travel experiences or those of colleagues or clients.

Sales and marketing skills are important to promote their services. Travel agents make presentations to social and special-interest groups, arrange advertising displays, and suggest company-sponsored trips to business managers. Depending on the size of the travel agency, an agent may specialize by type of travel, such as leisure or business, or destination, such as Europe or Africa.

Canada Cuba Education Tours & Trips

Edu Tours To Cuba.com is the number one Canada based coast-to-coast web site specializing in customized group educational and cultural trips to Cuba. Their travel agency is considered to be the largest in terms of both the variety and quantity of our tours, as well as the quality of our special trips. They have clients from all provinces. They also have escorted tours available which you can join.

Youth travel to Cuba based on friendship and exchange tours with the Cuban people is one of our main specialties.

They can organize a package of any kind to Cuba from Vancouver to the Maritimes: Calgary, Edmonton, Saskatoon, Regina, Winnipeg, Toronto, Ottawa, Montreal, Halifax, St. John, Moncton, St John's and others.

They work with all major airline companies including Air Canada, Cubana, and others such as Sky Service, Air Transat.

Air Canada offers Toronto to Havana direct flights; and so we can provide you and your group with a connector flight to Toronto from any city in Canada served by Air Canada.

EduToursToCuba.com knows Cuba and knows Canada. Take advantage of our experience and allow us to help you with your trip.

There seems to be distinct differences between those traveling on business and those traveling for pleasure. It is likely that you, as a reader of Utah Business, have experienced both business and leisure travel extensively.

You, like me, may relate to the horrendous experience which Steve Martin portrayed in the recent film "Planes, Trains, and Automobiles." You may experience cancellations due to weather, sitting next to someone who talks too much, worring about your towels being stolen, and so forth.

Business and leisure travelers do share one common goal--getting from point A to point B as quickly and safely as possible. Whether you travel primarily for business or pleasure, developing a good relationship with a reliable travel agent can save you time, money, and hassles.

FIND THE RIGHT AGENT

Travel agencies come in all shapes and sizes. Some specialize in leisure travel, some in group tours, some in business travel, but few do very well with all of it. Most of the services provided by travel agencies are provided at no additional cost to the traveler. They earn a commission from the vendor who provides the actual mode of transportation or accommodation.

The travel agencies' cut of the airline ticket is around 9 percent. The rest goes to the airline, the government, and credit-card companies. The same price is charged by the airline, whether the air tickets are distributed through a travel agency or not. More than 80 percent of all airline tickets are now distributed through travel agent.

Travel Agency

A travel agency is a retail business that sells travel related products and services to customers on behalf of suppliers such as airlines, car rentals, cruise lines, hotels, railways, sightseeing tours and package holidays that combine several products. In addition to dealing with ordinary tourists most travel agencies have a separate department devoted to making travel arrangements for business travelers and some travel agencies specialize in commercial and business travel only. There are also travel agencies that serve as general sales agents for foreign travel companies, allowing them to have offices in countries other than where their headquarters are located.

The British company Cox & Kings is sometimes said to be the oldest travel agency in the world, but this rests upon the services that the original bank, established in 1758, supplied to its wealthy clients. The modern travel agency first appeared in the second half of the 19th century. Thomas Cook, in addition to developing the package tour, established a chain of agencies in the last quarter of the 19th century, in association with the Midland Railway.

They not only sold their own tours to the public, but in addition, represented other tour companies. Other British pioneer travel agencies were Dean and Dawson, the Polytechnic Touring Association and the Co-operative Wholesale Society. The oldest travel agency in North America is Brownell Travel; on July 4, 1887, Walter T. Brownell led ten travelers on a European tour, setting sail from New York on the SS Devonia.

Travel agencies became more commonplace with the development of commercial aviation, starting in the 1920s. Originally, travel agencies largely catered to middle and upper class customers, but the post-war boom in mass-market package holidays resulted in travel agencies on the main streets of most British towns, catering to a working-class clientele, looking for a convenient way to book overseas beach holidays.

Operations

As the name implies, a travel agency's main function is to act as an agent, that is to say, selling travel products and services on behalf of a supplier. Consequently, unlike other retail businesses, they do not keep a stock in hand. A package holiday or a ticket is not purchased from a supplier unless a customer requests that purchase. The holiday or ticket is supplied to them at a discount.

The profit is therefore the difference between the advertised price which the customer pays and the discounted price at which it is supplied to the agent. This is known as the commission. A British travel agent would consider a 10-12% commission as a good arrangement. In Australia, all individuals or companies that sell tickets are required to be licensed as a travel agent.

In some countries, airlines have stopped giving commission to travel agencies. Therefore, travel agencies are now forced to charge a percentage premium or a standard flat fee, per sale. However, some companies still give them a set percentage for selling their product. Major tour companies can afford to do this, because if they were to sell a thousand trips at a cheaper rate, they still come out better than if they sell a hundred trips at a higher rate. This process benefits both parties.

Other commercial operations are undertaken, especially by the larger chains. These can include the sale of in-house insurance, travel guide books and timetables, car rentals, and the services of an on-site Bureau de change, dealing in the most popular holiday currencies.

The majority of travel agents have felt the need to protect themselves and their clients against the possibilities of commercial failure, either their own or a supplier's. They will advertise the fact that they are surety bonded, meaning in the case of a failure, the customers are guaranteed either an equivalent holiday to that which they have lost or if they prefer, a refund. Many British and American agencies and tour operators are bonded with the International Air Transport Association (IATA), for those who issue air tickets, Air Travel Organisers' Licensing (ATOL) for those who order tickets in, the Association of British Travel

Agents (ABTA) or the American Society of Travel Agents (ASTA), for those who sell package holidays on behalf of a tour company.

A travel agent is supposed to offer impartial travel advice to the customer. However, this function almost disappeared with the mass-market package holiday and some agency chains seemed to develop a 'holiday supermarket' concept, in which customers choose their holiday from brochures on racks and then book it from a counter. Again, a variety of social and economic changes have now contrived to bring this aspect to the fore once more, particularly with the advent of multiple, no-frills, low-cost airlines.

Commissions

Most travel agencies operate on a commission-basis, meaning that the compensation from the airlines, car rentals, cruise lines, hotels, railways, sightseeing tours and tour operators, etc., is expected in form of a commission from their bookings. Most often, the commission consists of a set percentage of the sale.

In the United States, most airlines pay no commission at all to travel agencies. In this case, an agency usually adds a service fee to the net price.

Types of Agencies

There are three different types of agencies in the UK: Multiples, Miniples and Independent Agencies. The former comprises a number of national chains, often owned by international conglomerates, like Thomson Holidays, now a subsidiary of TUI AG, the German multinational. It is now quite common for the large mass-market tour companies to purchase a controlling interest in a chain of travel agencies, in order to control the distribution of their product. (This is an example of vertical integration.) The smaller chains are often based in particular regions or districts.

In the United States, there are four different types of agencies: Mega, Regional, Consortium and Independent Agencies. American Express and the American Automobile Association (AAA) are examples of mega travel agencies.

Independent Agencies usually cater to a special or niche market, such as the needs of residents in an upmarket commuter town or suburb or a particular group interested in a similar activity, such as sporting events, like football, golf or tennis.

There are two approaches of travel agencies. One is the traditional, multi-destination, out-bound travel agency, based in the originating location of the traveler and the other is the destination focused, in-bound travel agency, that is based in the destination and delivers an expertise on that location. At present, the former is usually a larger operator like Thomas Cook, while the latter is often a smaller, independent operator.

Consolidators

Airline consolidators and other types of travel consolidators and wholesalers are high volume sales companies that specialize in selling to niche markets. They may or may not offer various types of services, at a single point of access. These can be hotel reservations, flights or car-rentals, for example. Sometimes the services are combined into vacation packages, that include transfers to the location and lodging.

These companies do not usually sell directly to the public, but act as wholesalers to retail travel agencies. Commonly, the sole purpose of consolidators is to sell to ethnic niches in the travel industry. Usually, no consolidator offers everything, they may only have contracted rates to specific destinations. Today, there are no domestic consolidators, with some exceptions for business class contracts.

CRITICISM AND CONTROVERSY

Travel agencies have been accused of employing a number of restrictive practices, the chief of which is known as 'racking'. This is the practice of displaying only the brochures of those travel companies whose holidays they wish to sell, the ones that pay them the most commission. Of course, the average customer tends to think that these are the only holidays on offer and is unaware of the possible alternatives.

Conversely, by limiting the number of companies that a travel agency represents, this can bring a better and more profitable, working relationship between the agency and its suppliers. Travel agencies can then obtain special benefits for their customers, from a supplier, by concentrating their bookings with that supplier. Some examples of these special benefits would be room upgrades or the waiver of change and cancellation fees.

Internet Threat

With general public access to the Internet, many airlines and other travel companies began to sell directly to passengers. As a consequence, airlines no longer needed to pay the commissions to travel agents on each ticket sold. Since 1997, travel agencies have gradually been disintermediated, by the reduction in costs caused by removing layers from the package holiday distribution network. However, travel agents remain dominant in some areas such as cruise vacations where they represent 77% of bookings and 73% of packaged travel.

In response, travel agencies have developed an internet presence of their own by creating travel websites, with detailed information and online booking capabilities. Several major online travel agencies include: Expedia, Voyages-sncf.com, Travelocity, Orbitz, CheapTickets, Priceline, CheapOair and Hotwire.com. Travel agencies also use the services of the major computer reservations systems companies, also known as Global Distribution Systems (GDS), including: SABRE, Amadeus CRS, Galileo CRS and Worldspan, which is a subsidiary of Travelport, allowing them to book and sell airline tickets, hotels, car rentals and other travel related services. Some online travel websites allow visitors to compare hotel and flight rates with multiple companies for free. They often allow visitors to sort the travel packages by amenities, price, and proximity to a city or landmark.

Travel agents have applied dynamic packaging tools to provide fully bonded (full financial protection) travel at prices equal to or lower than a member of the public can book online. As such, the agencies' financial assets are protected in addition to professional travel agency advice.

All travel sites that sell hotels online work together with GDS, suppliers and hotels directly to search for room inventory. Once the travel site sells a hotel, the site will try to get a confirmation for this hotel. Once confirmed or not, the customer is contacted with the result.

This means that booking a hotel on a travel website will not necessarily result in an instant answer. Only some hotels on a travel website can be confirmed instantly (which is normally marked as such on each site). As different travel websites work with different suppliers together, each site has different hotels that it can confirm instantly. Some examples of such online travel websites that sell hotel rooms are Expedia, Orbitz and WorldHotel-Link.

The comparison sites, such as Kayak.com, TripAdvisor and SideStep search the resellers site all at once to save time searching. None of these sites actually sell hotel rooms.

Often tour operators have hotel contracts, allotments and free sell agreements which allow for the immediate confirmation of hotel rooms for vacation bookings. Mainline service providers are those that actually produce the direct service, like various hotels chains or airlines that have a website for online bookings. Portals will serve a consolidator of various airlines and hotels on the internet.

They work on a commission from these hotels and airlines. Often, they provide cheaper rates than the mainline service providers as these sites get bulk deals from the service providers. A meta search engine on the other hand, simply culls data from the internet on real time rates for various search queries and diverts traffic to the mainline service providers for an online booking. These websites usually do not have their own booking engine.

Careers

With the many people switching to self-service internet websites, the number of available jobs as travel agents is decreasing. Most jobs that become available are from older travel agents retiring. Counteracting the decrease in jobs due to internet services is the increase in the number of people travelling. Since 1995, many travel agents have exited the industry, and relatively few young people have entered the field due to less competitive salaries.

However, others have abandoned the 'brick and mortar' agency for a home-based business to reduce overheads and those who remain have managed to survive by promoting other travel products such as cruise lines and train excursions or by promoting their ability to aggressively research and assemble complex travel packages on a moment's notice, essentially acting as a very advanced concierge. In this regard, travel agents can maintain competitive, if they become "travel consultants" with flawless knowledge of destination regions and specialize in topics like nautical tourism or cultural tourism.

Travel Technology

It is a term used to describe applications of Information Technology (IT), or Information and Communications

Technology (ICT), in travel, tourism and hospitality industry. Travel technology may also be referred to as tourism technology, hospitality automation, travel tracking and flight tracking.

Since travel implies locomotion, travel technology was originally associated with the computer reservations system (CRS) of the airlines industry, but now is used more inclusively, incorporating the broader tourism sector as well as its subset the hospitality industry. While travel technology includes the computer reservations system, it also represents a much broader range of applications, in fact increasingly so. Travel technology includes virtual tourism in the form of virtual tour technologies. Travel technology may also be referred to as e-travel / etravel or e-tourism / etourism (eTourism), in reference to "electronic travel" or "electronic tourism".

Travel technology is increasingly being used to describe systems for managing and monitoring travel, including travel tracking and flight tracking systems.

In other contexts, the term "travel technology" can refer to technology intended for use by travelers, such as light-weight laptop computers with universal power supplies or satellite Internet connections. That is not the sense in which it is used here.

APPLICATIONS OF TRAVEL TECHNOLOGY

Travel technology includes many processes such as dynamic packaging which provide useful new options for consumers. Today the tour guide can be a GPS tour guide, and the guidebook could be an audioguide, podguide or I-Tours, such as City audio guides. The biometric passport may also be included as travel technology in the broad sense.

XML-based technologies have become increasingly important for the travel industry. XML can be used to support air reservation booking or to implement optional services and merchandising functions in the booking process. Another important application of XML is the establishing of direct connections between Airlines and Travel Agencies. In order to create a generally accepted XML-standard, the Open Axis Group was founded.

Certainly travel technology was born on the coat-tails of the airline industry's use of automation and their need to extend this out to the travel agency partners. It should be kept in mind that there was an online world before the advent of the world wide web in the form of private and commercial online services, via packet switched network using X.25. Travel technology played a significant role in the so-called dot-com boom and bust, circa 1997-2001.

Electronic Ticket

An electronic ticket or e-ticket is used to represent the purchase of a seat on a passenger airline, usually through a website or by telephone, or sometimes through airline ticket offices or travel agencies. This form of airline ticket rapidly replaced the older multi-layered paper tickets (from close to zero to 100% in about 10 years) and became mandatory for IATA members as from June 1, 2008. During the last few years, where paper tickets were still available, airlines frequently charged extra for issuing them. E-tickets are also available for some entertainment venues.

Once a reservation is made, an e-ticket exists only as a digital record in the airline computers. Customers usually print out a copy of their receipt which contains the record locator or reservation number and the e-ticket number.

According to critical acclaim, Joel R. Goheen is recognized as the Inventor of Electronic Ticketing in the Airline Industry, an industry where global electronic ticket sales (the industry standard) accounts for over US$400 billion a year (2007). Electronic tickets have been introduced in road, urban or rail public transport as well.

Checking in with an e-ticket

To check in with an e-ticket, the passenger usually goes to the check-in counter and presents the e-ticket itinerary receipt which contains a confirmation or reservation code. In some airports and airlines it is not even necessary to present this document or quote the confirmation code or e-ticket number as the reservation is confirmed solely on the basis of the passenger's identity, which may be proven by a passport or the matching credit card. The rest of the check-in process remains the same as when paper tickets were the norm, that is, the passenger checks-in his/her luggage. The e-ticket is not a substitute for the boarding pass which must still be issued at the end of the check-in process.

Self-service and Remote check-in

E-tickets are very popular because they allow extra services like:

- online access to a passenger's reservation which makes amendments to flight plans (such as change of flight date and refunds) possible (subject to ticket restrictions)
- online/telephone/self-service kiosk check-in (if the airline makes this option available)
- early check-in
- printing boarding passes at airport kiosks and at locations other than an airport

It is also possible to have many copies of an e-ticket, hence the "loss" of an airline ticket becomes impossible.

Several web sites exist to help people holding e-tickets accomplish online check-ins in advance of the twenty-four-hour airline restriction. These sites store a passenger's flight information and then when the airline opens up for online check-in the data is transferred to the airline and the boarding pass is emailed back to the customer.

E-tickets are sometimes not available for some flights from an airline which usually offers them. This can be due to a number of reasons, the most common being software incompatibility. If an airline issues tickets for a codeshare flight with another company, and there is no e-ticket interlining agreement, the operating carrier would not be able to see the issuing carrier's ticket. Therefore, the carrier that books the flight needs to provide hard copy versions of the tickets so that the ticket can be processed. Similarly, if the destination airport does not have access to the airline who booked the flight, a paper ticket needs to be issued.

Currently the ticketing systems of most airlines are only able to produce e-tickets for itineraries of no more than 16 segments, including surface segments.

IATA Mandated Transition

As part of the IATA Simplifying the Business initiative, the association instituted a program to switch the industry to 100% electronic ticketing. The program concluded on June 1, 2008, with the association saying that the resulting industry savings were approximately US$3 billion.

In 2004, IATA Board of Governors set the end of 2007 as the deadline for airlines to make the transition to 100% electronic ticketing for tickets processed through the IATA billing and settlement plan; in June 2007, the deadline was extended to May 31, 2008.

As of June 1, 2008 paper tickets can no longer be issued on neutral stock by agencies reporting to their local BSP. Agents reporting to the ARC using company-provided stock or issuing tickets on behalf of an airline (GSAs and ticketing offices) are not subject to that restriction.The industry was unable to comply with the IATA mandate and paper tickets remain in circulation as of February 2009.

Digital Ticket

A digital ticket is a virtual instance of a ticket which represents the digitization of rights to claim goods or services. In order to make an implementation of the digital ticket system, a combination of two paradigms can be used. The first is the account-based system, which relies on central storage and network connections. The second is the smartcard-based system, which uses decentralized storage to store and transfer the ticket.

A digital ticket must fulfill the following criteria:

- Secure (unable to alter or counterfeit)
- Portable (physical independence)
- Off-line capable
- Wide acceptability (In order to have the ticket generally accepted, some level of trust is needed.)
- User-friendly

In addition, another three requirements are also important for digital tickets, they are:

Viewable

The terms and description of the service should be objectively understood by both the service provider and consumer or owner, so the value of the ticket can be determined. Moreover, this is an essential property to trace the digital ticket.

State Manageable

Tickets may also have a payment status, i.e., paid or unpaid, and/or reservation status, e.g., waiting list, reserved, or canceled. The status may be changed dynamically. In addition, the ticket ownership can be rewritten when the ticket is transferred. However, it is difficult to allow these changes while still guaranteeing security.

(De)Composable

Combining two or more tickets is sometimes required to obtain a service or one ticket may comprise several parts. For example, a travel ticket can comprise an accommodation ticket and a plane ticket or a car rent ticket.

Besides the criteria mentioned above, there are still several features that should be concerned, such as anonymity, transferability and repetitive usability.

Lifecycle

The ticket is first issued by the service provider or issuer. The ownership of a ticket may change after it was issued, by transferring the ticket. Either the issuer or owner of ticket might view the status of the ticket. Finally, it is redeemed by the current owner at the service provider.

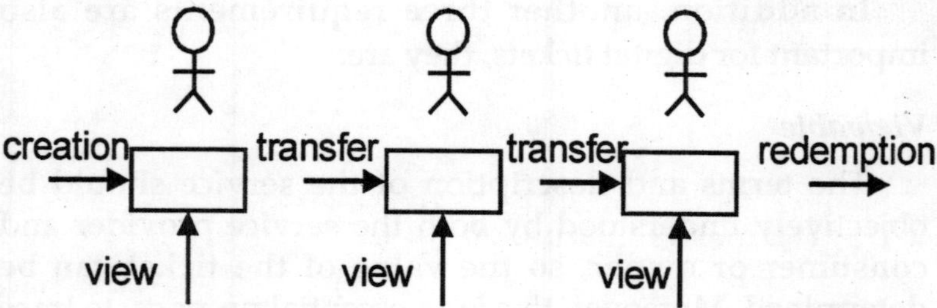

Creation

From creator's point of view, each digital ticket has certain structure, this could be expressed in a multilayer architecture depicted as follows:

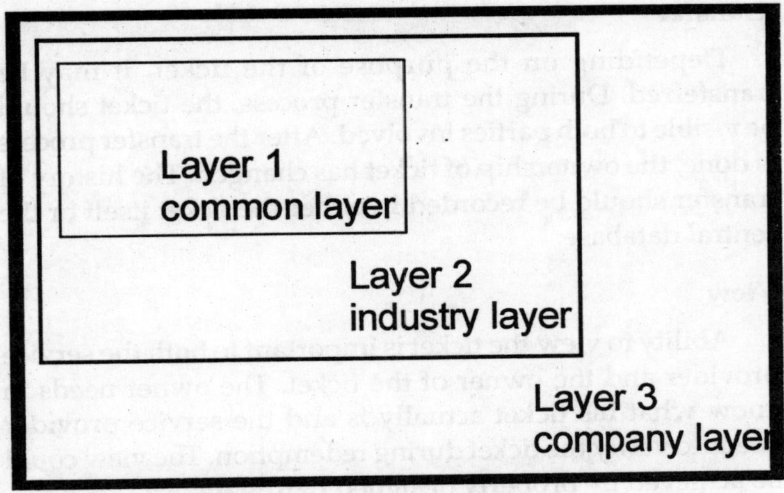

Layer 1

Common ticket properties that do not depend on the ticket type:

- Issuer
- Promise (Details are given in upper layers)
- Owner
- Transferability
- Number of times to be consumed
- Valid period
- View
- Issuer's signature on above

Layer 2

Ticket properties defined by each industry

Layer 3

Ticket properties defined by each issuing company or individual

Transfer

Depending on the purpose of the ticket, it may be transferred. During the transfer process, the ticket should be visible to both parties involved. After the transfer process is done, the ownership of ticket has changed. The history of transfer should be recorded in either the ticket itself or the central database.

View

Ability to view the ticket is important to both the service provider and the owner of the ticket. The owner needs to know what his ticket actually is and the service provider needs to verify the ticket during redemption. The view could be achieved by properly designed hardware.

Redemption

A digital ticket always has certain value that could be redeemed at service provider. Normally after redeeming, the ticket is cleaned. Some tickets work for a period, and will only be deleted after this period. In the special case when the ticket isn't given away after redeeming, it is called a pass.

Account-based System

In an account-based system for tickets the rights of the tickets are managed in accounts. Ticket changes in accounts can be made by communicating with a so-called account manager through a network. The trust in these systems can be seen from the service provider's and user's perspective, in which the former generally manages the whole system. This leads to an imbalanced trust relationship. Two other disadvantages of these systems are the need for protection of accounts against malicious users and the relatively large efforts that need to be done to store all the accounts for both the users and the service provider.

Storage

Generally the storage and maintaining tasks of the account are assigned to the service provider. This leads to costs and efforts on his side. In some cases these systems could be shared by different service providers, but a need to make general agreements remains. Since the service provider normally has full control over the accounts, tickets could be deleted or altered and after that refuse to fulfill the service the initial ticket stands for.

Authentication

Typically ID and password are used in account-based systems to authenticate a user. This does not prevent fraud by the service provider. Several digital-cash systems deal with this by having a secret key generated at the user's PC, which remains out of hands of the service provider. This however is not sufficient when tickets are redeemed at the real service provider.

Prevention of Duplicate Redemption

Since the account management is completely in control of the service providers, unwanted actions such as copying tickets can easily be detected and traced back by them.

Smart card-based System

In smart card-based systems, tickets are stored on a smart card and are circulated by putting two smart cards in a reader and completing the transaction. The smart card itself takes care of the calculations that need to be done for safe transferring.

Storage

Tickets are stored on the smart cards. The smart cards can be provided by both the users and the service providers. The performance of current smart cards is limited, which makes asynchronous trading difficult. Different service providers are likely to use different standards, which makes it mandatory to have a different smart cards for different kinds of tickets.It is very useful to passengers.

Authentication

A secret key can be implemented in the smart card, which makes it possible to carry the card around and redeem a ticket without using a network connection. When the service provider distributes and issues the private keys on these cards, fraud from malicious service providers is still an issue. This also makes it hard for different service providers to share a smart card.

PREVENTION OF DUPLICATE REDEMPTION

Storage is generally maintained by the service provider. The smart card needs to be protected against multiplication. However, if the system is broken security is completely lost.

e-cash

Using cryptography, e-cash was introduced by David Chaum as an anonymous electronic cash system. He used blind signatures to achieve unlinkability between withdrawal and spend transactions. Depending on the properties of the payment transactions, one distinguishes between on-line and off-line electronic cash. The first off-line e-cash system was proposed by Chaum and Naor. Like the first on-line method, it is based on RSA blind signatures.

In the United States, only one bank implemented ecash, the Mark Twain bank, and the system was dissolved in 1997 after the bank was purchased by Mercantile Bank, a large issuer of credit cards. Similar to credit cards, the system was free to purchasers, while merchants paid a transaction fee.

In Australia ecash was implemented by The St. Georges Bank, but the transactions were not free to purchasers. In June 1998, ecash became available through Credit Suisse in

Switzerland. It was also available from Deutsche Bank in Germany, Bank Austria, Finland's Merita Bank/Eunet, Sweden's Posten, and Den norske Bank of Norway.

Chapter–5

ROLE OF GLOBALIZATION

The term is most closely associated with the term economic globalization: the integration of national economies into the international economy through trade, foreign direct investment, capital flows, migration, the spread of technology, and military presence. However, globalization is usually recognized as being driven by a combination of economic, technological, sociocultural, political, and biological factors.

The United Nations ESCWA says globalization "is a widely-used term that can be defined in a number of different ways. When used in an economic context, it refers to the reduction and removal of barriers between national borders in order to facilitate the flow of goods, capital, services and labour... although considerable barriers remain to the flow of labor... Globalization is not a new phenomenon. The term can also refer to the transnational circulation of ideas, languages, or popular culture through acculturation. An aspect of the world which has gone through the process can be said to be globalized.

Globalization describes the process by which regional economies, societies, and cultures have become integrated through a global network of political ideas through communication, transportation, and trade.

Government officials and different national and International organizations are studying the impact of globalization on various aspects of life in India including its impact on Indian culture, value system and employment but the most important aspect being neglected is "Has it any impact on rural life", where more than 60 percent of Indian population resides.International and national organizations are trying to study its impact on various aspects of life in general.

Basic facilities: Impact is clearly visible on urban life but rural life in India has not changed much. If we start from the basic facilities, impact is not so marked as in urban areas. People are still living in houses made of mud barring houses of few rich and progressive farmers. Government made houses for people in the name of "Indira Awaas Yojna" are so poorly designed and constructed that a family of three to four people can not live comfortably in these houses. Occupation has been taken by the people but most of them are still staying in their earlier made "Kuchcha " houses. Conditions of farming communities are yet untouched from globalization. Laborers' conditions have somewhat improved due to implementation of "Minimum Wages by the Government.

Prime Minister Rojgar Yojna and CM Rojgar Yojna have made partial employment available to this segment. Government has initiated several developmental programs for uplift of living standards of people but full benefits have not reached to the targeted population due to corruption prevalent in administrative and political systems. Pradhan Mantri Gramin Sadak Yojna has resulted in road connectivity in rural India but roads are of poor quality and without drainage support. Toilet and lavatory systems are not of standard quality and not even constructed in all houses of the village. Even today more than 90 percent people in villages attend the call of nature in open fields.

Electricity: Life in rural India is miserable due to non-availability of electricity. Several states in India claim that 40, 50 or even 100 percent villages have been electrified. But supply of electricity to villages that have been electrified is not more than 3-4 hours per day. It is big hindrance in development. Globalization is not going to make much difference to rural life until ad unless electricity is supplied uninterruptedly 10-12 hours per days too these villages.

Education: School buildings are available in few villages but number of teachers is inadequate in primary schools. Benches, boards and other facilities are of sub-standard quality. There is, however, one positive development that girls are attending the schools in the villages. Also the number of students attending graduate and post graduate courses is increasing but awareness among students from rural areas lacks towards technical education and that is the single reason that most of the students from rural areas are unable to secure employment.

Technology: Technology has failed to percolate to villages in absence of electricity and other communication infrastructure. Few people know about the internet. However, well-to-do families have availed DTH and dish TV facilities. Mobile connections are increasing in rural areas but at slower pace. There are no small scale industries in villages to provide employment to educated youth.

Culture and social values: India's real culture is still preserved in rural life. New advancement of technology has not much influence in rural areas. People still prefer to wear dresses of old fashion and celebrate festivals in old styles. Folk dances and folk songs are still popular among villagers. Culture is still untouched and unaffected by western influence. Globalization has no impact on rural life as standards of living are suboptimal but migration of people is taking place and poor people are moving to urban areas in search of employment.

Agriculture: Globalization does not have any positive impact on agriculture. On the contrary, it has few deterimental effect as government is always willing to import food grains, sugar etc whenever there is a price increase of these commodities. Government never thinks to pay more to farmers so that they produce more food grains but resorts to imports. On the other hand, subsidies are declining so cost of production is increasing. Even forms producing fertilizers have to suffer due to imports. There are also threats like introduction of GM crops, herbicide resistant crops etc.

Tom G. Palmer of the Cato Institute defines globalization as "the diminution or elimination of state-enforced restrictions on exchanges across borders and the increasingly integrated and complex global system of production and exchange that has emerged as a result."

Thomas L. Friedman has examined the impact of the "flattening" of the world, and argues that globalized trade, outsourcing, supply-chaining, and political forces have changed the world permanently, for both better and worse. He also argues that the pace of globalization is quickening and will continue to have a growing impact on business organization and practice.

Herman E. Daly argues that sometimes the terms internationalization and globalization are used interchangeably but there is a significant formal difference. The term "internationalization" (or internationalisation) refers to the importance of international trade, relations, treaties etc. owing to the (hypothetical) immobility of labor and capital between or among nations.

Finally, Takis Fotopoulos argues that globalization is the result of systemic trends manifesting the market economy's grow-or-die dynamic, following the rapid expansion of transnational corporations. Because these trends have not been offset effectively by counter-tendencies that could have emanated from trade-union action and other forms of political activity, the outcome has been globalization. This is a multi-faceted and irreversible phenomenon within the system of the market economy and it is expressed as: economic globalization, namely, the opening and deregulation of commodity, capital and labour markets which led to the present form of neoliberal globalization; political globalization, i.e., the emergence of a transnational elite and the phasing out of the all powerful nation-state of the statist period; cultural globalization, i.e., the worldwide homogenisation of culture; ideological globalization; technological globalization; social globalization.

Effects Summary

Globalization has various aspects which affect the world in several different ways

- Industrial - emergence of worldwide production markets and broader access to a range of foreign products for consumers and companies. Particularly movement of material and goods between and within national boundaries. International trade in manufactured goods increased more than 100 times (from $95 billion to $12 trillion) in the 50 years since 1955. China's trade with Africa rose sevenfold during 2000-07 alone.
- Financial - emergence of worldwide financial markets and better access to external financing for borrowers. By the early part of the 21st century more than $1.5 trillion in national currencies were traded daily to support the expanded levels of trade and investment. As these worldwide structures grew more quickly than any transnational regulatory regime, the instability of the global financial infrastructure dramatically increased, as evidenced by the Financial crisis of 2007-2010.
- Economic - realization of a global common market, based on the freedom of exchange of goods and

capital. The interconnectedness of these markets, however, meant that an economic collapse in one area could impact other areas. With globalization, companies can produce goods and services in the lowest cost location. This may cause jobs to be moved to locations that have the lowest wages, least worker protection and lowest health benefits. For Industrial activities this may cause production to move to areas with the least pollution regulations or worker safety regulations.

Almost all notable worldwide IT companies have a presence in India. Four Indians were among the world's top 10 richest in 2008, worth a combined $160 billion. In 2007, China had 415,000 millionaires and India 123,000.

- Job Market- competition in a global job market. In the past, the economic fate of workers was tied to the fate of national economies. With the advent of the information age and improvements in communication, this is no longer the case. Because workers compete in a global market, wages are less dependent on the success or failure of individual economies. This has had a major effect on wages and income distribution.
- Health Policy - On the global scale, health becomes a commodity. In developing nations under the demands of Structural Adjustment Programs, health systems are fragmented and privatized. Global health policy makers have shifted during the 1990s from United Nations players to financial institutions. The result of this power transition is an increase in privatization in the health sector. This privatization fragments health policy by crowding it with many players with many private interests. These fragmented policy players emphasize partnerships and specific interventions to combat

specific problems (as opposed to comprehensive health strategies). Influenced by global trade and global economy, health policy is directed by technological advances and innovative medical trade. Global priorities, in this situation, are sometimes at odds with national priorities where increased health infrastructure and basic primary care are of more value to the public than privatized care for the wealthy.

- Political - some use "globalization" to mean the creation of a world government which regulates the relationships among governments and guarantees the rights arising from social and economic globalization. Politically, the United States has enjoyed a position of power among the world powers, in part because of its strong and wealthy economy. With the influence of globalization and with the help of the United States' own economy, the People's Republic of China has experienced some tremendous growth within the past decade. If China continues to grow at the rate projected by the trends, then it is very likely that in the next twenty years, there will be a major reallocation of power among the world leaders. China will have enough wealth, industry, and technology to rival the United States for the position of leading world power.

Among the political effects some scholars also name the transformation of sovereignty. In their opinion, 'globalization contributes to the change and reduction of nomenclature and scope of state sovereign powers, and besides it is a bilateral process: on the one hand, the factors are strengthening that fairly undermine the countries' sovereignty, on the other - most states voluntarily and deliberately limit the scope of their sovereignty'.

- Informational - increase in information flows between geographically remote locations. Arguably this is a technological change with the advent of fibre optic communications, satellites, and increased availability of telephone and Internet.
- Language - the most popular first language is Mandarin (845 million speakers) followed by Spanish (329 million speakers) and English (328 million speakers). However the most popular second language is undoubtedly English, the "lingua franca" of globalization:
  - o About 35% of the world's mail, telexes, and cables are in English.
  - o Approximately 40% of the world's radio programs are in English.
  - o English is the dominant language on the Internet.
- Competition - Survival in the new global business market calls for improved productivity and increased competition. Due to the market becoming worldwide, companies in various industries have to upgrade their products and use technology skillfully in order to face increased competition.
- Ecological - the advent of global environmental challenges that might be solved with international cooperation, such as climate change, cross-boundary water and air pollution, over-fishing of the ocean, and the spread of invasive species. Since many factories are built in developing countries with less environmental regulation, globalism and free trade may increase pollution and impact on precious fresh water resources(Hoekstra and Chapagain 2008). On the other hand, economic development historically required a "dirty" industrial stage, and it is argued that developing countries should not, via regulation,

be prohibited from increasing their standard of living.

London is a city of considerable diversity. As of 2008, estimates were published that stated that approximately 30% of London's total population was from an ethnic minority group. The latest official figures show that in 2008, 590,000 people arrived to live in the UK whilst 427,000 left, meaning that net inward migration was 163,000.

- Cultural - growth of cross-cultural contacts; advent of new categories of consciousness and identities which embodies cultural diffusion, the desire to increase one's standard of living and enjoy foreign products and ideas, adopt new technology and practices, and participate in a "world culture". Some bemoan the resulting consumerism and loss of languages. Also see Transformation of culture.
  - o Spreading of multiculturalism, and better individual access to cultural diversity (e.g. through the export of Hollywood). Some consider such "imported" culture a danger, since it may supplant the local culture, causing reduction in diversity or even assimilation. Others consider multiculturalism to promote peace and understanding between people. A third position that gained popularity is the notion that multiculturalism to a new form of monoculture in which no distinctions exist and everyone just shift between various lifestyles in terms of music, cloth and other aspects once more firmly attached to a single culture. Thus not mere cultural assimilation as mentioned above but the obliteration of culture as we know it today. In reality, as it happens in countries like the United Kingdom, Canada, Australia or New Zealand, people who always lived in their native countries maintain their cultures without

feeling forced by any reason to accept another and are proud of it even when they're acceptive of immigrants, while people who are newly arrived simply keep their own culture or part of it despite some minimum amount of assimilation, although aspects of their culture often become a curiosity and a daily aspect of the lives of the people of the welcoming countries.

- Greater international travel and tourism. WHO estimates that up to 500,000 people are on planes at any one time. In 2008, there were over 922 million international tourist arrivals, with a growth of 1.9% as compared to 2007.
- Greater immigration, including illegal immigration. The IOM estimates there are more than 200 million migrants around the world today. Newly available data show that remittance flows to developing countries reached $328 billion in 2008.
- Spread of local consumer products (e.g., food) to other countries (often adapted to their culture).
- Worldwide fads and pop culture such as Pokémon, Sudoku, Numa Numa, Origami, Idol series, YouTube, Orkut, Facebook, and MySpace; accessible only to those who have Internet or Television, leaving out a substantial portion of the Earth's population.
- Worldwide sporting events such as FIFA World Cup and the Olympic Games.
- Incorporation of multinational corporations into new media. As the sponsors of the All-Blacks rugby team, Adidas had created a parallel website with a downloadable interactive rugby game for its fans to play and compete.

- Social - development of the system of non-governmental organisations as main agents of global public policy, including humanitarian aid and developmental efforts.
- Technical
  - o Development of a Global Information System, global telecommunications infrastructure and greater transborder data flow, using such technologies as the Internet, communication satellites, submarine fiber optic cable, and wireless telephones
  - o Increase in the number of standards applied globally; e.g., copyright laws, patents and world trade agreements.
- Legal/Ethical
  - o The creation of the international criminal court and international justice movements.
  - o Crime importation and raising awareness of global crime-fighting efforts and cooperation.
  - o The emergence of Global administrative law.
- Religious
  - o The spread and increased interrelations of various religious groups, ideas, and practices and their ideas of the meanings and values of particular spaces.

Cultural Effects

"Culture" is defined as patterns of human activity and the symbols that give these activities significance. Culture is what people eat, how they dress, the beliefs they hold, and the activities they practice. Globalization has joined different cultures and made it into something different.

Culinary culture has become extensively globalized. For example, Japanese noodles, Swedish meatballs, Indian curry,

French cheese, and American burgers and fries have become popular outside their countries of origin. Two American companies, McDonald's and Starbucks, are often cited as examples of globalization, with over 31,000 and 18,000 locations operating worldwide, respectively.

Another common practice brought about by globalization is the usage of Chinese characters in tattoos. These tattoos are popular with today's youth despite the lack of social acceptance of tattoos in China. Also, there is a lack of comprehension in the meaning of Chinese characters that people get, making this an example of cultural appropriation.

The internet breaks down cultural boundaries across the world by enabling easy, near-instantaneous communication between people anywhere in a variety of digital forms and media. The Internet is associated with the process of cultural globalization because it allows interaction and communication between people with very different lifestyles and from very different cultures. Photo sharing websites allow interaction even where language would otherwise be a barrier.

ECONOMIC LIBERALIZATION

According to Jagdish Bhagwati, a former adviser to the U.N. on globalization, although there are obvious problems with overly-rapid development, globalization is a very positive force that lifts countries out of poverty. According to him, it causes a virtuous economic cycle associated with faster economic growth.

Workers in developing countries now have more occupational choices then ever before. Educated workers in developing countries are able to compete on the global job market for high paying jobs. Production workers in developing countries are not only able to compete, they have a strong advantage over their counterparts in the industrialized world. This translates into increased opportunity. Workers have the choice of emigrating and taking jobs in industrial countries or staying at home to work in outsourced industries. In addition, the global economy provides a market for the products of cottage industry, providing more opportunities.

Globalization has generated significant international opposition over concerns that it has increased inequality and environmental degradation. In the Midwestern United States, globalization has eaten away at its competitive edge in industry and agriculture, lowering the quality of life.

Some also view the effect of globalization on culture as a rising concern. Along with globalization of economies and trade, culture is being imported and exported as well. The concern is that the stronger, bigger countries such as the United States, may overrun the other, smaller countries' cultures, leading to those customs and values fading away. This process is also sometimes referred to as Americanization or McDonaldization.

JOBS

Income Inequality

The globalization of the job market has had negative consequences in developed countries. "Mind workers" (engineers, attorneys, scientists, professors, executives, journalists, consultants) are able to compete successfully in the world market and command high wages. Conversely, production workers and service workers in industrialized nations are unable to compete with workers in third world countries and either lose their jobs through outsourcing or are forced to accept wage cuts.

This has resulted in a growing gap between the incomes of the rich and poor. This trend seems to be greater in the United States than other industrial countries. Income inequality in the United States started to rise in the late

1970,'s, however the rate of increase rose sharply in the 21st century; it has now reached a level comparable with that found in developing countries.

Brain Drains

Opportunities in rich countries drives talent away from poor countries, leading to brain drains. Brain drain has cost the African continent over $4.1 billion in the employment of 150,000 expatriate professionals annually. Indian students going abroad for their higher studies costs India a foreign exchange outflow of $10 billion annually.

Sweatshops

In many poorer nations, globalization is the result of foreign businesses utilizing workers in a country to take advantage of the lower wage rates.

One example used by anti-globalization protestors is the use of sweatshops by manufacturers. According to Global Exchange these "Sweat Shops" are widely used by sports shoe manufacturers and mentions one company in particular - Nike. There are factories set up in the poor countries where employees agree to work for low wages. Then if labour laws alter in those countries and stricter rules govern the manufacturing process the factories are closed down and relocated to other nations with more business favorable policies, such as Cambodia or Bangladesh.

There are several agencies that have been set up worldwide specifically designed to focus on anti-sweatshop campaigns and education of such. In the USA, the National Labor Committee has proposed a number of bills as part of Decent Working Conditions and Fair Competition Act, which have thus far failed in Congress. The legislation would legally require companies to respect human and worker rights by prohibiting the import, sale, or export of sweatshop goods.

Specifically, these core standards include no child labor, no forced labor, freedom of association, right to organize and bargain collectively, as well as the right to decent working conditions.

There are also concerns about the emergence of "electronic sweatshops." Shehzad Nadeem writes that the outsourcing of service work, such as customer service and Information Technology work, to India has resulted in "longer work hours, an intense work pace, and temporal displacement manifested in health problems and alienation from family and friends."

Natural Resources

Air

The Worldwatch Institute said the booming economies of China and India are planetary powers that are shaping the global biosphere. In 2007, China overtook the United States as the world's biggest producer of CO_2. Only 1 percent of the country's 560 million city inhabitants (2007) breathe air deemed safe by the European Union.

Forests

A major source of deforestation is the logging industry, driven spectacularly by China and Japan. China and India are quickly becoming large oil consumers. China has seen oil consumption grow by 8% yearly since 2002, doubling from 1996-2006. State of the World 2006 report said the two countries' high economic growth hid a reality of severe pollution. The report states:

The world's ecological capacity is simply insufficient to satisfy the ambitions of China, India, Japan, Europe and the United States as well as the aspirations of the rest of the world in a sustainable way

At present rates, tropical rainforests in Indonesia would be logged out in 10 years, Papua New Guinea in 13 to 16 years.

Minerals

Without more recycling, zinc could be used up by 2037, both indium and hafnium could run out by 2017, and terbium could be gone before 2012. It is said that if China and India were to consume as much resources per capita as United States or Japan in 2030 together they would require a full planet Earth to meet their needs. In the longterm these effects can lead to increased conflict over dwindling resources and in the worst case a Malthusian catastrophe.

Food

The head of the International Food Policy Research Institute, stated in 2008 that the gradual change in diet among newly prosperous populations is the most important factor underpinning the rise in global food prices. From 1950 to 1984, as the Green Revolution transformed agriculture around the world, grain production increased by over 250%. The world population has grown by about 4 billion since the beginning of the Green Revolution and most believe that, without the Revolution, there would be greater famine and malnutrition than the UN presently documents (approximately 850 million people suffering from chronic malnutrition in 2005).

It is becoming increasingly difficult to maintain food security in a world beset by a confluence of "peak" phenomena, namely peak oil, peak water, peak phosphorus, peak grain and peak fish. Growing populations, falling energy sources and food shortages will create the "perfect storm" by 2030, according to the UK government chief scientist. He said food reserves are at a 50-year low but the world requires 50% more energy, food and water by 2030.

The world will have to produce 70% more food by 2050 to feed a projected extra 2.3 billion people and as incomes rise, the United Nations' Food and Agriculture Organisation (FAO) warned. Social scientists have warned of the possibility that global civilization is due for a period of contraction and economic re-localization, due to the decline in fossil fuels and resulting crisis in transportation and food production. One paper even suggested that the future might even bring about a restoration of sustainable local economic activities based on hunting and gathering, shifting horticulture, and pastoralism.

In 2003, 29% of open sea fisheries were in a state of collapse. The journal Science published a four-year study in November 2006, which predicted that, at prevailing trends, the world would run out of wild-caught seafood in 2048.

Health

Further Information: Globalization and Disease

Globalization has also helped to spread some of the deadliest infectious diseases known to humans. Starting in Asia, the Black Death killed at least one-third of Europe's population in the 14th century. Even worse devastation was inflicted on the American supercontinent by European arrivals. 90% of the populations of the civilizations of the "New World" such as the Aztec, Maya, and Inca were killed by small pox brought by European colonization. Modern modes of transportation allow more people and products to travel around the world at a faster pace, but they also open the airways to the transcontinental movement of infectious disease vectors. One example of this occurring is AIDS/HIV. Due to immigration, approximately 500,000 people in the United States are believed to be infected with Chagas disease. In 2006, the tuberculosis (TB) rate among foreign-born persons in the United States was 9.5 times that of U.S.-born persons.

Global Market

Expansion

A flood of consumer goods such as televisions, radios, bicycles, and textiles into the United States, Europe, and

Japan has helped fuel the economic expansion of Asian tiger economies in recent decades. However, Chinese textile and clothing exports have recently encountered criticism from Europe, the United States and some African countries. In South Africa, some 300,000 textile workers have lost their jobs due to the influx of Chinese goods. The increasing U.S. trade deficit with China has cost 2.4 million American jobs between 2001 and 2008, according to a study by the Economic Policy Institute (EPI). A total of 3.2 million - one in six U.S. factory jobs - have disappeared between 2000 and 2007.

A report issued in 2007 by PricewaterhouseCoopers LLP predicted that by 2050 the economies of the E7 emerging economies (the BRIC countries: China, India, Brazil, and Russia, plus Indonesia and Turkey) will be around 50% larger than the current G7 (US, Japan, Germany, UK, France, Italy and Canada). China is expected to overtake the US as the largest economy around 2025, while India will overtake the US in 2050. A more recent report isued by Goldman Sachs that was compiled after China released their GDP growth figures for 2009 predicted that China is about to overtake Japan and may become the world's largest economy by 2020.

Financial Interdependency

The world today is so interconnected that the collapse of the subprime mortgage market in the U.S. has led to a global financial crisis and recession on a scale not seen since the Great Depression. According to critics, government deregulation and failed regulation of Wall Street's investment banks were important contributors to the subprime mortgage crisis.

Since the mid-1970s, it has been argued that geographic diversification would eventually generate superior risk-adjusted returns for long-term global investors by reducing overall portfolio risk while capturing some of the higher rates of return offered by emerging markets. By doing so, these institutional investors have contributed to the financial and economic development of key nations in Asia, Eastern Europe and Latin America. Typically, for global investors, India and China constitute both large-scale production platforms and reservoirs of new consumers, whereas Russia is viewed essentially as an exporter of oil and commodities-Brazil and Latin America being somehow "in the middle".

Drug and Illicit Goods Trade

The United Nations Office on Drugs and Crime (UNODC) issued a report that the global drug trade generates more than $320 billion a year in revenues. Worldwide, the UN estimates there are more than 50 million regular users of heroin, cocaine and synthetic drugs. The international trade of endangered species is second only to drug trafficking. Traditional Chinese medicine often incorporates ingredients from all parts of plants, the leaf, stem, flower, root, and also ingredients from animals and minerals. The use of parts of endangered species (such as seahorses, rhinoceros horns, saiga antelope horns, and tiger bones and claws) has created controversy and resulted in a black market of poachers who hunt restricted animals. In recent years, debates about globalization have tended to descend into polemics and confusion as opinions have become increasingly politicized. There is little common ground between proponents and opponents of globalization.

Politicization of the Debate in the United States

The study by Peer Fiss and Paul Hirsch suggests that the politicization of this discourse has emerged largely in response to greater US involvement with the international economy. For example, their survey shows that in 1993 more than 40% of respondents were unfamiliar with the concept of globalization. When the survey was repeated in 1998, 89% of the respondents had a polarized view of globalization as being either good or bad. At the same time, discourse on globalization, which was at first confined largely to the financial community, started to focus instead on an increasingly heated debate between proponents of globalization and a dipartite group of disenchanted students and workers. Polarization increased dramatically after the establishment of the WTO in 1995; this event and subsequent protests led to a large-scale anti-globalization movement.

Their study shows that, the neutral frame was the dominant frame in newspapers articles and corporate press releases prior to 1989. Both media depicted globalization as a natural development that related to technological advancement. In 1986, for example, nearly 90% of newspaper articles exhibited neutral framing. The situation started to change after the collapse of the stock market in Oct.19, 1987 and the subsequent recession. Newspapers began to voice concerns about the trend toward "globalization" and the interconnectedness of international financial markets. By 1989, the number of positively and negatively framed articles had eclipsed the number of neutrally framed articles. By 1998, neutrally framed articles had been reduced to 25% of the total.

The study also shows an especially large increase in the number of negatively framed articles. Prior to 1995, positively framed articles were more common than negatively framed articles, however, by 1998, the number of negatively framed articles was double that of positively framed articles. A recent article in the Wall Street Journal suggests that this rise in opposition to globalization can be explained, at least in part, by economic self-interest.

Initially, college educated workers were the most likely to support globalization. Less educated workers, who were more likely to compete with immigrants and workers in developing countries, tended to oppose globalization. The situation changed radically when white collar workers started to blame immigration and globalization for their own increased economic insecurity. According to a poll conducted for the Wall Street Journal and NBC News, in 1997, 58% of college graduates said globalization had been good for the U.S. while 30% said it had been bad. When the poll asked a similar question in 2008 (after the financial crisis of 2007), 47% of graduates thought globalization was bad and only 33% thought it was good. Respondents with high school education, who were always opposed to globalization, became more opposed.

The Debate in Other Industrialized Countries

Philip Gordon, in a recent article in Yale Global, states that "(as of 2004) a clear majority of Europeans believe that globalization can enrich their lives, while believing the European Union can help them take advantage of globalization's benefits while shielding them from its negative effects." The main opposition consists of left-wing socialists, environmental groups, and right-wing nationalists.

Part of the reason for the difference in response to globalization in US and EU lies in the fact that workers in the US have been more strongly impacted by factors like automation and outsourcing than their European counterparts. Income Inequality in the US, for example, is now much higher than in the EU. Gordon points out that workers in the EU feel less threatened by globalization. First, the job market in the EU is more stable than that of the US, and workers in the EU are less likely to accept wage cuts or loss of benefits. Second, social spending by governments in the EU is much higher than in the US. The situation is very different in the US, where there is a strong sense of individualism.

In Japan, the debate takes a different form. According to Takenaka Heizo and Chida Ryokichi, there is a perception that the economy is "Small and Frail", which seems ironic in a country that accounts for one-quarter of all production. However Japan is resource poor and must promote exports in order to import the raw materials it needs. Anxiety over their position has caused terms like internationalization and globalization to become part of everyday language in Japan. The Japanese accept that internationalization and globalization cannot be avoided. However, their resource dependency requires them to be as self-sufficient as possible in sectors like agriculture. Most discourse, therefore, centers on the notion of self-sufficiency.

The situation may have changed after the financial crisis of 2007. A recent BBC World Public Poll taken between October 31, 2007 and January 25, 2008, suggests that opposition to globalization in industrialized countries may be increasing. Unfortunately, it is difficult to compare the results with the polls mentioned above; those polls asked whether the overall effect of globalization was good or bad, whereas the BBC poll asked whether globalization was growing too rapidly. The countries where people are most likely say that globalization is growing too fast are France, Spain, Japan, South Korea, and Germany. There is even the suggestion that the trend in these countries is even stronger than in the United States. The poll also correlates the tendency to view globalization as proceeding too rapidly with a perception of growing economic insecurity and social inequality.

The Debate in the Developing World

A number of international polls have shown that residents of developing countries tend to view globalization more favorably than residents of the US or the EU However, a recent poll undertaken by the BBC indicates that there is a growing feeling in the Third World that globalization is proceeding too rapidly. There are only a few countries, including Mexico, the countries of Central America, Indonesia, Brazil and Kenya, where a majority felt that globalization is growing too slowly.

Many in the Third World see globalization is a positive force that lifts countries out of poverty. The opposition often combines environmental concerns with nationalism. Governments are often seen as agents of neo-colonialism that open the doors to an invasion of multinational corporations. Much of this criticism comes from the established middle class; a report from the Brookings Institute suggests this is because the middle class perceive upwardly-mobile low-income groups to be a threat to their economic security.

Although many critics blame globalization for a decline of the middle class in industrialized countries, a recent report in The Economist suggests that the middle class is growing rapidly in the Third World. Unfortunately, this growth, coupled with growing urbanization, has led to increasing disparities in wealth between urban and rural areas. This leads to a situation where those who have gained the least economically have the most to lose from the negative environmental impact of globalization. For example, in India 70% of the population lives in rural areas and depend directly on access to natural resources for their livelihood. As a result, anti-globalization often takes the form of mass movements in the countryside.

The situation is critical in China, where rapid growth has led to a situation where 0.4% of the population possess 70% of the nation's wealth. An 2007 article in The Economist blamed increaing unrest in rural China on the growing gap in wealth between rural and urban areas. This, plus growing worker discontent in industrialized areas,. has caused a great deal of concern among the nation's leadership

Alternative ways of Interpreting Discourse on Globalization

The analysis presented above focuses on the politicization of discourse and the way politically motivated actors represent globalization to the public; it is more interested in the process of politicization than in the meanings of globalization. It is also possible to examine discourse on globalization in terms of these meanings and their implications for the understanding issues like national autonomy and sovereignty.

For example, David Held and Anthony McGrew, in an article in The Oxford Companion to Politics of the World, have suggested that this discourse can be separated into three frames. 1) Hyperglobalists hold that autonomy and sovereignty of nation-states have been eclipsed by contemporary processes of economic globalization. 2) Sceptics hold that intensity of contemporary global interdependence is considerably exaggerated and that the hyperglobalists ignore the continued primacy of national power and sovereignty. 3) Transformationalists emphasize the way in which globalization has brought about the spatial re-organization and re-articulation of economic, political, military and cultural power.

Peer Fiss and Paul Hirsch, in an article on the discourse of globalization, suggested using the notion of framing as a way to study this polarization. By framing, they mean the way "interested actors and entrepreneurs articulate particular versions of reality to potential supporters..." They identified three main frames:

1. The positive frame points to the potential gains and benefits of globalization.
2. The neutral frame portrays globalization as a natural, evolutionary, and largely inevitable development. This discourse, which is associated with the financial community, avoids making moral judgments.
3. The negative frame points out the increasing potential for economic crisis, the threat to the livelihoods of workers, and the growing income inequality caused by globalization. This frame also includes discourse which is primarily concerned with the negative impact of globalization in the Third World.

To which we should add a fourth, newly emergent frame:

4. The constructive frame is an emerging frame that is more positive and constructive than the negative frame. This discourse supports global cooperation and interaction while opposing some of the negative effects of globalization

The Positive Frame: Advocates of Globalization

1. Neo-Liberalism

The majority of books, newspaper articles and press releases in this frame represent the neo-liberal view of globalization. Supporters of free trade claim that it increases economic prosperity as well as opportunity, especially among developing nations, enhances civil liberties and leads to a more efficient allocation of resources. Economic theories of comparative advantage suggest that free trade leads to a more efficient allocation of resources, with all countries involved in the trade benefiting. In general, this leads to lower prices, more employment, higher output and a higher standard of living for those in developing countries.

Proponents of laissez-faire capitalism, and some libertarians, say that higher degrees of political and economic freedom in the form of democracy and capitalism in the developed world are ends in themselves and also produce higher levels of material wealth. They see globalization as the beneficial spread of liberty and capitalism.

Supporters of democratic globalization are sometimes called pro-globalists. They believe that the first phase of globalization, which was market-oriented, should be followed by a phase of building global political institutions representing the will of world citizens. The difference from other globalists is that they do not define in advance any ideology to orient this will, but would leave it to the free choice of those citizens via a democratic process.

2. *The Global Village*

An optimistic view of globalism is suggested by Marshall McLuhan's of the Global Village This view suggests that globalization will lead to a world where people from all countries will become more integrated and aware of common interests and shared humanity.

3. *The Importance of International Cooperation*

A third body of literature points out the value of international cooperation in solving problems of mutual concern ranging from human-rights issues to environmental concerns such as global warming. This view is similar to that represented by the constructive frame.

4. *World Government*

Dr. Francesco Stipo, Director of the United States Association of the Club of Rome, writes in favor of political globalization in the form of a world government, suggests that it "should reflect the political and economic balances of world nations. A world confederation would not supersede the authority of the State governments but rather complement it, as both the States and the world authority would have power within their sphere of competence".

Some, such as former Canadian Senator Douglas Roche, O.C., simply view globalization as inevitable and advocate creating institutions such as a directly elected United Nations Parliamentary Assembly to exercise oversight over unelected international bodies.

The Neutral Frame: The Practical Approach

This involves a form of discourse that portrays globalization as a natural, evolutionary, and largely inevitable development. This type of discourse, which is characteristic of the financial community, has become less prominent as the issue of globalization has become increasingly politicized. For example, a study of newspaper articles has shown that the percentage of articles exhibiting neutral framing decreased from nearly 90% in 1986 to around 25% in 1998. It should be noted, however, that the number of newspaper articles dealing with globalization increased almost tenfold during that period. Therefore, the total number of neutral articles has probably increased.

Examples of literature associated with this frame would include textbooks, books on international finance, and articles on globalization found in financial journals like the Wall Street Journal.

The Negative Frame: Critics of Globalization

Since 1991, this discourse has been increasing rapidly in importance in the United states; the number of newspaper articles showing negative framing rose from about 10% of the total in 1991 to 55% of the total in 1999. This increase occurred during a period when the total number of articles concerning globalization nearly doubled. This discourse takes two very different forms:

1. Concern over economic well being in developed countries

In industrialized countries discourse about globalization centers on economic self-interest. Newspaper articles about globalization typically express concerns involve the interconnectedness of international financial markets and the potential for economic crisis, as well as threats to the livelihood of workers\.

2. Concern over the impact of globalization in developing countries

The establishment of the WTO in 1995 and subsequent protests led to a large-scale anti-globalization movement that is primarily concerned with the negative impact of globalization in developing countries. Their concerns range from environmental issues to issues like democracy, national sovereignty and the exploitation of workers.

Individuals who associate themselves with the anti-globalization movement in industrialized countries comprise a relatively small but vocal minority. They are overwhelmingly upper middle-class, college-educated elites. This contrasts sharply with the situation in developing countries, where the anti-globalization movement has been more successful in achieving a broader, more balanced social class composition, with millions of workers and farmers getting actively involved.

The Constructive Frame: Finding Common Ground

This discourse involves a synthesis combining elements of all three of the above forms. It is practical, insofar as it accepts the reality of international integration and attempts to work within it. It is positive in that it believes that international cooperation can provide solutions to important problems. At the same time, it recognizes the negative aspects of globalization and proposes ways to mitigate their impact.

Beginning in 2001 with the World Social Forum (WSF), there has been a movement consisting of individuals trying to bring about this type of synthesis. It is associated with the term Alter-globalization (or altermondialization), a positive spin on the term anti-globalization. Members of this movement support the international integration of globalization, but demand that values of democracy, economic justice, environmental protection, and human rights be put ahead of purely economic concerns. This movement is discussed at length in the section Alter-globalization.

The Anti-globalization Movement

"Anti-globalization" can involve the process or actions taken by a state or its people in order to demonstrate its sovereignty and practice democratic decision-making. Anti-globalization may occur in order to maintain barriers to the international transfer of people, goods and beliefs, particularly free market deregulation, encouraged by business organizations and organizations such as the International Monetary Fund or the World Trade Organization. Moreover, as Naomi Klein argues in her book No Logo, anti-globalism can denote either a single social movement or an umbrella term that encompasses a number of separate social movements such as nationalists and socialists.

In either case, participants stand in opposition to the unregulated political power of large, multi-national corporations, as the corporations exercise power through leveraging trade agreements which in some instances create unemployment, and damage the democratic rights of citizens, the environment particularly air quality index and rain forests , as well as national government's sovereignty to determine labor rights, including the right to form a union, and health and safety legislation, or laws as they may otherwise infringe on cultural practices and traditions of developing countries.

Some people who are labeled "anti-globalist" or "sceptics" (Hirst and Thompson) consider the term to be too vague and inaccurate. Podobnik states that "the vast majority of groups that participate in these protests draw on international networks of support, and they generally call for forms of globalization that enhance democratic representation, human rights, and egalitarianism."

Joseph Stiglitz and Andrew Charlton write:

"The anti-globalization movement developed in opposition to the perceived negative aspects of globalization. The term 'anti-globalization' is in many ways a misnomer, since the group represents a wide range of interests and issues and many of the people involved in the anti-globalization movement do support closer ties between the various peoples and cultures of the world through, for example, aid, assistance for refugees, and global environmental issues."

Some members aligned with this viewpoint prefer instead to describe themselves as the "Global Justice Movement", the "Anti-Corporate-Globalization Movement", the "Movement of Movements" (a popular term in Italy), the "Alter-globalization" movement (popular in France), the "Counter-Globalization" movement, and a number of other terms.

Critiques of the current wave of economic globalization typically look at both the damage to the planet, in terms of the perceived unsustainable harm done to the biosphere, as well as the perceived human costs, such as poverty, inequality, miscegenation, injustice and the erosion of traditional culture which, the critics contend, all occur as a result of the economic transformations related to globalization. They challenge directly the metrics, such as GDP, used to measure progress promulgated by institutions such as the World Bank, and look to other measures, such as the Happy Planet Index, created by the New Economics Foundation. They point to a "multitude of interconnected fatal consequences-social disintegration, a breakdown of democracy, more rapid and extensive deterioration of the environment, the spread of new diseases, increasing poverty and alienation" which they claim are the unintended but very real consequences of globalization.

The terms globalization and anti-globalization are used in various ways. Noam Chomsky believes that:

- The term "globalization" has been appropriated by the powerful to refer to a specific form of international economic integration, one based on investor rights, with the interests of people incidental. That is why the business press, in its more honest moments, refers to the "free trade agreements" as "free investment agreements" (Wall St. Journal). Accordingly, advocates of other forms of globalization are described as "anti-globalization"; and some, unfortunately, even accept this term, though it is a term of propaganda that should be dismissed with ridicule. No sane person is opposed to globalization, that is, international integration. Surely not the left and the workers movements, which were founded on the principle of international solidarity - that is, globalization in a form that attends to the rights of people, not private power systems.

- The dominant propaganda systems have appropriated the term "globalization" to refer to the specific version of international economic integration that they favor, which privileges the rights of investors and lenders, those of people being incidental. In accord with this usage, those who favor a different form of international integration, which privileges the rights of human beings, become "anti-globalist." This is simply vulgar propaganda, like the term "anti-Soviet" used by the most disgusting commissars to refer to dissidents. It is not only vulgar, but idiotic. Take the World Social Forum, called "anti-globalization" in the propaganda system - which happens to include the media, the educated classes, etc., with rare exceptions. The WSF is a paradigm example of globalization. It is a gathering of huge numbers of people from all over the world, from just about every corner of life one can think of, apart from the extremely narrow highly privileged elites who meet at the competing World Economic Forum, and are called "pro-globalization" by the propaganda system. An observer watching this farce from Mars would collapse in hysterical laughter at the antics of the educated classes.

Critics argue that globalization results in:

- Poorer countries suffering disadvantages: While it is true that globalization encourages free trade among countries, there are also negative consequences because some countries try to save their national markets. The main export of poorer countries is usually agricultural goods. Larger countries often subsidise their farmers (like the EU Common Agricultural Policy), which lowers the market price for the poor farmer's crops compared to what it would be under free trade.
- The exploitation of foreign impoverished workers: The deterioration of protections for weaker nations by stronger industrialized powers has resulted in the exploitation of the people in those nations to become cheap labor. Due to the lack of protections, companies from powerful industrialized nations are able to offer workers enough salary to entice them to endure extremely long hours and unsafe working conditions, though economists question if consenting workers in a competitive employers' market can be decried as "exploited". It is true that the workers are free to leave their jobs, but in many poorer countries, this would mean starvation for the worker, and possible even his/her family if their previous jobs were unavailable.
- The shift to outsourcing: Globalization has allowed corporations to move manufacturing and service jobs from high cost locations to locations with the lowest wages and worker benefits. This results in loss of jobs in the high cost locations. This has contributed to the deterioration of the middle class which is a major factor in the increasing economic inequality in the United States . Families that were once part of the middle class are forced into lower positions by massive layoffs and outsourcing to

another country. This also means that people in the lower class have a much harder time climbing out of poverty because of the absence of the middle class as a stepping stone.

- Weak labor unions: The surplus in cheap labor coupled with an ever growing number of companies in transition has caused a weakening of labor unions in the United States. Unions lose their effectiveness when their membership begins to decline. As a result unions hold less power over corporations that are able to easily replace workers, often for lower wages, and have the option to not offer unionized jobs anymore.
- An increase in exploitation of child labor: for example, a country that experiencing increases in labor demand because of globalization and an increase the demand for goods produced by children, will experience greater a demand for child labor. This can be "hazardous" or "exploitive", e.g., quarrying, salvage, cash cropping but also includes the trafficking of children, children in bondage or forced labor, prostitution, pornography and other illicit activities.

In December 2007, World Bank economist Branko Milanovic has called much previous empirical research on global poverty and inequality into question because, according to him, improved estimates of purchasing power parity indicate that developing countries are worse off than previously believed. Milanovic remarks that "literally hundreds of scholarly papers on convergence or divergence of countries' incomes have been published in the last decade based on what we know now were faulty numbers." With the new data, possibly economists will revise calculations, and he also believed that there are considerable implications estimates of global inequality and poverty levels. Global inequality was estimated at around 65 Gini points, whereas the new numbers indicate global inequality to be at 70 on the Gini scale.

The critics of globalization typically emphasize that globalization is a process that is mediated according to corporate interests, and typically raise the possibility of alternative global institutions and policies, which they believe address the moral claims of poor and working classes throughout the globe, as well as environmental concerns in a more equitable way.

The movement is very broad , including church groups, national liberation factions, peasant unionists, intellectuals, artists, protectionists, anarchists, those in support of relocalization and others. Some are reformist, (arguing for a more moderate form of capitalism) while others are more revolutionary (arguing for what they believe is a more humane system than capitalism) and others are reactionary, believing globalization destroys national industry and jobs.

One of the key points made by critics of recent economic globalization is that income inequality, both between and within nations, is increasing as a result of these processes. One article from 2001 found that significantly, in 7 out of 8 metrics, income inequality has increased in the twenty years ending 2001. Also, "incomes in the lower deciles of world income distribution have probably fallen absolutely since the 1980s". Furthermore, the World Bank's figures on absolute poverty were challenged. The article was skeptical of the World Bank's claim that the number of people living on less than $1 a day has held steady at 1.2 billion from 1987 to 1998, because of biased methodology.

A chart that gave the inequality a very visible and comprehensible form, the so-called 'champagne glass' effect, was contained in the 1992 United Nations Development Program Report, which showed the distribution of global income to be very uneven, with the richest 20% of the world's population controlling 82.7% of the world's income.

Distribution of World GDP, 1989

Quintile of Population	Income
Richest 20%	82.7%
Second 20%	11.7%
Third 20%	2.3%
Fourth 20%	2.4%
Poorest 20%	0.2%

Source: United Nations Development Program. 1992 Human Development Report

Economic arguments by fair trade theorists claim that unrestricted free trade benefits those with more financial leverage (i.e. the rich) at the expense of the poor.

Americanization related to a period of high political American clout and of significant growth of America's shops, markets and object being brought into other countries. So globalization, a much more diversified phenomenon, relates to a multilateral political world and to the increase of objects, markets and so on into each others countries.

Critics of globalization talk of Westernization. A 2005 UNESCO report showed that cultural exchange is becoming more frequent from Eastern Asia but Western countries are still the main exporters of cultural goods. In 2002, China was the third largest exporter of cultural goods, after the UK and US. Between 1994 and 2002, both North America's and the European Union's shares of cultural exports declined, while Asia's cultural exports grew to surpass North America. Related factors are the fact that Asia's population and area are several times that of North America.

Some opponents of globalization see the phenomenon as the promotion of corporatist interests. They also claim that the increasing autonomy and strength of corporate entities shapes the political policy of countries.

WAYS OF MEASUREMENT

Economic globalization can be measured in different ways. This center around the four main economic flows that characterize globalization:

- Goods and services, e.g., exports plus imports as a proportion of national income or per capita of population
- Labor/people, e.g., net migration rates; inward or outward migration flows, weighted by population
- Capital, e.g., inward or outward direct investment as a proportion of national income or per head of population
- Technology, e.g., international research & development flows; proportion of populations (and rates of change thereof) using particular inventions (especially 'factor-neutral' technological advances such as the telephone, motorcar, broadband)

As globalization is not only an economic phenomenon, a multivariate approach to measuring globalization is the recent index calculated by the Swiss think tank KOF. The index measures the three main dimensions of globalization: economic, social, and political. In addition to three indices measuring these dimensions, an overall index of globalization and sub-indices referring to actual economic flows, economic restrictions, data on personal contact, data on information flows, and data on cultural proximity is calculated.

Data is available on a yearly basis for 122 countries, as detailed in Dreher, Gaston and Martens (2008). According to the index, the world's most globalized country is Belgium, followed by Austria, Sweden, the United Kingdom and the Netherlands. The least globalized countries according to the KOF-index are Haiti, Myanmar, the Central African Republic and Burundi.

A.T. Kearney and Foreign Policy Magazine jointly publish another Globalization Index. According to the 2006 index, Singapore, Ireland, Switzerland, the Netherlands, Canada and Denmark are the most globalized, while Indonesia, India and Iran are the least globalized among countries listed.

INTERNATIONAL SOCIAL FORUM

The slogan of the forum was "Another World Is Possible". It was here that the WSF's Charter of Principles was adopted to provide a framework for the fora.

The WSF became a periodic meeting: in 2002 and 2003 it was held again in Porto Alegre and became a rallying point for worldwide protest against the American invasion of Iraq. In 2004 it was moved to Mumbai, India, to make it more accessible to the populations of Asia and Africa. This last appointment saw the participation of 75,000 delegates.

Regional fora took place following the example of the WSF, adopting its Charter of Principles. The first European Social Forum was held in November 2002 in Florence. The slogan was "Against the war, against racism and against neo-liberalism". It saw the participation of 60,000 delegates and ended with a huge demonstration against the war of 1,000,000 people according to the organizers. The other two ESFs took place in Paris and London, in 2003 and 2004 respectively.

Recently there has been some discussion behind the movement about the role of the social forums. Some see them as a "popular university", an occasion to make many people aware of the problems of globalization. Others would prefer that delegates concentrate their efforts on the coordination and organization of the movement and on the planning of new campaigns. However it has often been argued that in the dominated countries (most of the world) the WSF is little more than an 'NGO fair' driven by Northern NGOs and donors most of which are hostile to popular movements of the poor.

CHAPTER–6

EXPLORING NATURE-BASED EDUCATIONAL TOURISM

Nature-Based Tourism is a large and growing industry sector in many destinations across the world. A wide range of recreational, activity based, educational, cultural activities and experiences, can be accessed by visitors in natural and protected areas. The development of natural and/or protected areas for tourism products and experiences requires a careful balance between providing adequate visitor experiences and services, protecting the ecological and cultural values of the area and ensuring the long-term sustainability of the site. Key considerations for the development of nature-based tourism include:

The development of tourism in natural and/or protected areas requires a careful balance between quality visitor experiences and services, protecting the ecological and cultural values of the area and ensuring the long-term sustainability of the site.

- Development of collaborative public / private partnerships for the identification of tourism development opportunities, understanding planning and development regulations and the management of visitors in the natural area; as demonstrated by the partnerships between Kakadu

National Park Management and commercial tour operators to ensure sustainable operations are developed.

- Understanding the political, social, cultural demographic and ecological environment surrounding the natural area when identifying potential tourism opportunities;
- Alignment with the park management plan and the park management objectives and goals in developing a tourism operation;
- Development of visitor education and interpretative information to provide an enhanced visitor experience and encourage conservation education;
- Working with the public sector to develop clear development and operational guidelines to ensure sustainable practices;
- Developing effective environmental management practices for tourism operations in natural areas.

The Sustainable Tourism Cooperative Research Centre has undertaken extensive research into tourism development in natural and protected areas. Further information on nature-based tourism can be found in the 'Parks and Culture' section.

In the early 1980s, ecotourism was initially connected with outdoor travel to remote, unique and/or scenic areas. Early ecotourism usually involved an educational or retreat focus. As ecotourism has increased in popularity, these educational elements became increasingly important. The recognized ecotourism industry has developed an organized framework for planning, management and economics.

The encompassing methodology considers the immediate environment, site-specific information including historic human use, conservation and preservation education, community responsibility and equitable social benefits; as well as outdoor activities and education. Ecotourism has been described to include pursuits as diverse as bicycling, bird watching, big-game hunting, meditation, sailing, paddling canoe trails, hiking and visits to buffalo farms, historic reenactments and museums.

Ecotourism and agritourism have many parallels and some development professionals consider the latter a subset of the former. In either case, much of the experience is designed around an area's natural variety, including its animal, plant and human cultural diversity. However, some adherents take exception with many of the activities of agritourism (for example, traditional farming and preserve-type hunting operations) if they are seen to be unsustainable or environmentally or culturally intrusive.

In general, ecotourism includes several major principles that should be a part of any basic business plan: education about the area; sustainable resource use, no environmental degradation; local community enhancement and assistance in the area's overall sustainable development; respect for the local people's cultural/social/political concerns; and profit for the business and the area's overall tourism industry.

When ecotourism is considered a component of rural development, its underlying concepts closely parallel those of modern rural-development and business planners. The underlying philosophy of rural development has changed from what was simply dumping any business "in the country" toward models for sustainable local development. The latter approach seeks to consider the development process in light of pressing community problems and issues and tries to directly address the most pressing reasons for under-development.

This concern for community and sustainable development is echoed in modern ecotourism thinking. Any sustainable business or community development should consider both overall community development; as well as a targeted group-approach to planning and problem solving. Participatory "buy in" from local and state government and engaged members of the community is a necessity.

This approach recognizes the full gamut of rural-society sociology: interrelationship between social groups, social institutions and taboos, political economy of the rural social structure, dynamics of social change, human relations and social environment, identities and locations of rural women in the development process, micro-financing and participation of marginal communities in development practices, contemporary and future rural development strategies, rural-urban migration; institutions for rural development and the reasons for and effects of participation of government and Private Voluntary Development Organizations (PVDOs) and private and public Non-Governmental Organizations (NGOs) in the development process. The old saying "No man (person) is an island," obviously applies to whether one is considering an overall development model for a community or a business model for an ecotourism venture within that community. Each reflects the identity of the other.

For example, most ecotourism in an agricultural context will be a farm-based agriculture-education or on-farm experience. This could be an activity like a corn maze, farm bed and breakfast or a visit to a northern-state sugarbush where maple syrup is produced (reduced) from tree sap. All of these reflect the cultural identity of the local area. Is it possible to make money off of what is right out your back door? Some enterprising individuals have done so by combining their love and knowledge of the out-of-doors with sound business planning and a vision for sharing this with others within and outside the local community.

A simple Internet search will find businesses based on the operator's love of birds and wildlife, agroforestry and permacultural education, to local farming museums and hunting and fishing operations. Many are centerpiece examples of ecotourism education programs that stress local natural character, history and the potential of the landscape. The key to these businesses is that they are driven by individuals who know the subject, enjoy communicating their knowledge to others while striving to make any visit an enjoyable experience the client will want to repeat.

So what are other ideas for these types of businesses? Again, a survey of any successfully vibrant rural community or general Internet search will produce ideas and identify activities that can inspire part or all of an ecotourism project. For example, a 2008 New York Times article on novel, innovative ecotourism projects and the future of ecotourism on the upper Great Plains suggested that it is the upscale consumer interested in novel experience that drives the industry. This article mentioned aircraft and off-road plains and bad-lands tours, bison hunts, wolf-watching and week-long birding expeditions with accommodations ranging from austere to five-star lodging. Of course, there are many others:

- Nature center with an emphasis on retreats or local-history, perhaps with catering or a local-craft outlet;
- Managed habitats and natural habitats and the role of trees and plants of the landscape: identification, speciation and co-evolution with insects, birds and mammals; plant identification (elementary taxonomy: major families and unique specific attributes); great naturalists in history; the concepts of xerascaping, agroforestry and permaculture; succession and the natural forest, prairie or riparian habitat;
- Outdoor educational demonstrations and hands-on activities that involve birds: falconry demonstrations, bird banding; birdhouses building, blinds and hides, properly using optics;

- Outdoor educational demonstrations and hands-on activities that involve area pre-history: Native-American pottery from hand-quarried clay and clam shells, flint-knapping, atlatls, fire-making with bow-drills;
- Outdoor educational demonstrations and hands-on activities that involve fishing and entomology or watercraft: fly-casting, fly tying and the dynamics of aquatic environments and the hydrosphere, kayak and canoe rentals and guided trips;
- Outdoor cooking: "gathering" (natural products from field to table), organic gardening;
- Outdoor team-building exercises or skill development (traditional canoe and kayak making, snowshoe making, shelter construction, winter-camping);
- Equine ecotourism (exploration on horseback, equestrian-skill training);
- Modern art from the landscape: weaving, photography, painting and sculpture workshops;
- Other activities: yoga, meditation, spiritual development, literature or history "of place" workshops.

Any exploration of a business venture should include a rigorous self-assessment. The individuals involved need to survey their capabilities, resources and potential time commitments. More involved business planning should include a SWOT (Strengths, Weaknesses, Opportunities and Threats) analysis. These need not be unnecessarily complicated and are relatively quick and easy to do. The object of the exercise is to examine the general feasibility of your idea. Models and templates can be found elsewhere on AgMRC or other business-development sites.

In the course of your planning activities, you should define your product and then gauge your market with respect to what other entities compete for the client's entertainment dollar. Critically judge the quality and value of the product that you intend to bring to the table and then consider whether your "competition" are really competitors or potential cooperators. If you are in any way contemplating educational or immersion-type experience programs, since many people have relatively short attention spans, be sure that your program moves along with ample hands-on participatory activities, especially if children are involved. Additionally, be sure that your operational plan contains risk-management contingencies for travel delays, bad weather and medical emergencies; and that some of these policies are clearly stated in writing in initial communications with the client.

Finally, look to the future. How do you plan to grow or at what level do you wish to comfortably sustain this business? What will by your eventual exit or succession strategy? Remember, you are not alone; network to find the assistance and information that you need. There are many local, state and national small-business resources that include Internet sites like AgMRC that include entrepreneur- and small-business-related discussion groups with links to and directories of public- and private-development specialists. There also are state and regional, Native-American, guide-outfitter, bed and breakfast, and similar tourism organizations.

EDUCATION TOURISM IN AFRICA

In Africa, education tourism or edu-tourism refers to any "programme in which participants travel to a location as a group with the primary purpose of engaging in a learning experience directly related to the location". It is comprised of several sub-types including ecotourism, heritage tourism, rural/farm tourism, and student exchanges between educational institutions. The notion of traveling for educational purposes is not new and its popularity in the tourism market is only expected to increase both locally and abroad. Victoria safaris is eager to increase its tourism earnings by tapping into this growing market phenomenon.

We take you to East Africa where we know and understand best in these resources. These resources may be categorized into the following dimensions in Kenya and East Africa as a whole:

Educational Tourism

These include; Agro tourism in western Kenya, community and cultural tours in Kenya, studying aquaculture in relation to Nile Perch, Tilapia and catfish in lake Victoria to discover their ecological limits; monitoring flamingoes(birds) migration in Kenya to restore declining populations and manage habitat change; tracking the habitats of rare endemic carnivores-the African lion and leopard; measuring the impact of public health education and clinical testing of intestinal parasites of remote villages around lake Victoria ; surveying traditional herbalists to preserve indigenous knowledge in the western Kenya region; a geographical, wildlife clubs, tourism clubs, agricultural shows and health club tours in Kenya are part of these resources.

Community, Cultural and Historical Education Tourism

This tour takes you to the communities Cultural and themes. These include: The culture of the luos around Lake Victoria, the culture of the Masai in the Kenya -Tanzania borders, arts and crafts of the western Kenya people, old architectural drawings and the old buildings in the cities of Kenya, Uganda and Tanzania, different African languages, archaeological sites, music, dance, slave trade, etc. Markets for Education Tourism in Sub-Sahara Africa.

Ecotourism and Nature Based Educational Tourism

Ecotourism involves visiting natural areas with the objectives of learning, studying or participating in activities that do not bring negative effects to the environment; whilst protecting and empowering the local community socially and economically. We consider an Eco Tour to be a trip that causes minimal impact to the environment and local people. The site is usually culturally and biologically diverse and attracts tourists and students who have a common interest in nature, wildlife and culture.

By choosing to go on an Eco Tour you will be given a unique opportunity to learn and experience nature. In addition a greater awareness of environmental issues will be developed as well as learning practices that can be incorporated in to your everyday routine on return. A fundamental element of an Eco Tour is the education of environmental issues such as, the protection of natural resources or endangered species, usually relevant to the destination. This may be conducted through lectures, involvement in conservation projects or simply by learning from our knowledgeable tour guides.

Rural Educational Tourism in Africa

The concept of Rural Educational Tourism is a direct expansion of ecotourism, which encourages visitors to experience rural cultural life at first hand. Rural Tourism is gathering strong support from small communities as rural people have realized the benefits of sustainable development brought about by similar forms of nature travel. Rural Educational tourism is a mild form of sustainable tourist development and multi-activity in rural areas through which the visitor/student has the opportunity to get acquainted with agricultural areas, agricultural occupations, local products, traditional cuisine and the daily life of the people, as well as the cultural elements and the authentic features of the area, while showing respect for the environment and tradition. Moreover, this activity brings visitors closer to nature and rural activities in which they can participate, be entertained and feel the pleasure of touring, learning and discovering. At the same time, it mobilizes the productive, cultural and developmental forces of an area, contributing in this way to the sustainable environmental, economic and social development of the rural area. Victoria safaris will take you for this tour.

Study Abroad Programs for Foreign Visitors

Victoria Safaris offers undergraduate students a unique opportunity to study in East Africa throughout the year. This program aims at preparing culturally-sensitive and diverse-thinking individuals from various academic and cultural backgrounds who are committed to experiential cross-cultural learning.

Student Cross Cultural Exchange programme in Kenya; This takes students to Western Kenya to the land of the Luos of central Nyanza who have traditionally subsisted on fishing and small scale farming. Students will be placed in individual home stays where they will begin to explore issues of tradition vs. modernity, change and continuity in socio-economic practices, and community vs state in a capitalist state. Here they immerse themselves in the daily life and ritual of their host community and work with locals on projects chosen by community leaders. They stay in homesteads in the rural village in Kenya where they will eat local foods, sleep in a local rural homestead, herd cattle ,use oxen plough, ride bicycles to the market, attend market days, and other village chores. Through hard work, they begin to understand and appreciate the problems and joys of living in a developing country. Those seeking overseas voluntary work and volunteer opportunities abroad will discover the difference one individual can make.

Whether you find yourself teaching English in a school in Africa, building a community center, or tending to village daily chores in Kenya, one thing is certain: this overseas voluntary work experience will change your life. These are a transformative experience to remember and to grow on. All student exchange programs end with 6 to 10 days spent exploring the environment and culture of the surrounding country. On these adventures, you might visit the Lake Victoria wildlife sanctuaries and the Maasai Mara national reserve, Ndere Island national park and Kakamega forest. Our high school summer programs are designed both for adventure and reflection. This final period of your high school programme offers you an opportunity to reflect on the experience and how you will integrate it into your life back home.

The student exchange programme is a two to three week home stay in a remote rural village. We can extend this program as per the demands of the students or the programme organisers. Our high school summer programs allow a maximum of 18 students per group; have two leaders and two to three in-country support staff.

Urbanization and Change in Kenya

This takes students to Nairobi, the capital city of Kenya where they will examine developmental and environmental issues that are both experienced and caused by the urban space. Students will meet and discuss with a selection of Nairobians their understanding and interpretation of the impact globalization has to them and their city. An urban home stay component will be used to integrate these discussions and interpretations into practical knowledge.

Wildlife Conservation and Ecology in Kenya

This will allow students to experience first-hand the wonders of Kenya's renowned wildlife heritage in the Maasai Mara while exploring the complex challenges faced by the traditional Maasai communities living in wildlife protected areas. Students will be encouraged to discuss with their hosts the intricate relationship that exists between a traditional society that has managed to fend off the beckoning of westernization and state machinery that seeks to embrace westernization at all costs.

ISLAM AND TOURISM IN MOMBASA

In this final part of the programme students will have an opportunity to live and interact with an urban Muslim community in Mombasa-the Swahili. Students will examine the critical role tourism plays in the economy and lives of Swahili people of Mombasa. They will learn about the challenges of balancing tourism, conservation in Old Town, and the fragile local Muslim culture.

Higher Educational Travel in Africa

Ontdek Kenya organizes educational travel and tours for high schools, colleges, universities and alumni associations that are seeking quality and truly nature based academic study tours that go beyond the morning and afternoon safaris game drives.

School trips are not just a fad in Ontdek's offering - teaching and all matters educational run deep with us as one of the directors, Anne, is a secondary school teacher by training with practical classroom experience. She has taught agriculture and sciences for 5 yrs to 14-18 yrs students.

It is with this background and our experience of organizing safaris since 1996, that we invite you to entrust us with your educational travel in Africa, because we clearly connect with your students educational needs.

We work hard to design school field trips that have soft activities, keep students away from mass tourism and at the same time raise their intellectual curiosity making them question the "Whys" of the world around them.

Ontdek has made a deliberate decision to offer educational tours strictly in Kenya, meaning we can maintain the high standards for which we are known for.

Contact Ontdek Kenya Safaris for a tailor-made high school trips to Kenya.

What makes Ontdek's students travel to Kenya unique?

- For the Teacher
- For the Student

In choosing an outfitter for your educational travel in Africa it matters that you pick one who shares your interest and is of course reliable. Ontdek Kenya fits this bill and we invite you to consider traveling with us. We look forward to consulting with you for your Kenya school tour.

Safari

A safari is an overland journey, usually a trip by tourists to Africa, traditionally for a big-game hunt; today the term often refers to a trip taken not for the purposes of hunting, but to observe and photograph animals and other wildlife. There is a certain theme or style associated with the word, which includes khaki clothing, belted bush jackets, pith helmets or slouch hats, and animal skins-like leopard's skin.

Entering the English language in the late 19th century, the word safari means "long journey" in Swahili. These words are used for any type of journey, e.g. by bus from Nairobi to Mombasa. The person generally attributed to having used the word in English is Sir Richard Francis Burton, the famous explorer.

The Regimental March of the King's African Rifles was 'Funga Safari', literally 'Halt the March', or, in other words, stop work for the day.

Funga safari, funga safari. Funga safari, funga safari. Hamari ya nani? Hamari ya nani? Hamari ya Bwana Kapteni, Hamari ya keyaa.

Which is, in English: Halt the march. Halt the march. On whose orders? On whose orders? On the order of the boss captain, On the order of the KAR.

On Kenya's independence from Britain, Funga Safari was retained as the Regimental March of the Kenya Rifles, successor to the K.A.R.

As a Cinema Genre

The safari provided countless hours of cinema entertainment in sound films from Trader Horn (1931) onwards. The safari was used in many adventure films such as the Tarzan, Jungle Jim, and Bomba the Jungle Boy film series up to The Naked Prey (1966) where Cornel Wilde, a white hunter, becomes game himself. Also, safaris and the safari genre films were parodied in the Bob Hope comedies Road to Zanzibar and Call Me Bwana.

An instant 15-minute helicopter safari was shown in Africa Addio where clients are armed, flown from their hotel and landed in front of an unlucky and baffled elephant. Out of Africa has Karen Blixen and Denys Finch Hatton travelling with Denys refusing to abandon home comforts using fine china and crystal and listening to Mozart recordings over the gramophone while on safari.

CHAPTER–7

CULTURAL EDUCATIONAL TOURISM

Russia is a country of richest history and culture. The most different religious and cultural traditions of numerous nationalities living there have coexisted from time immemorial.The architectural ensemble of Moscow Kremlin, palaces of Saint Petersburg, and ancient cities of the Golden Ring are known all over the world.

Moscow is the capital of the Russian Federation, and the business, scientific, cultural and tourist centre of Russia.

The first mention of Moscow dates back to 1147. The city was founded by Suzdal prince Jury Dolgoruky (Long-armed). Fast development of Moscow was promoted by its favorable geographical position at a crossing of major trading ways, between the rivers Oka and Volga on the Moskva-river. The architectural shape of the capital city has been formed for centuries.

Best Russian and foreign architects and artists worked in Moscow to create its unique image. Today Moscow is one of the most beautiful capitals in the world. Unique flavour is given to the city by the architectural complex of the Moscow Kremlin, the majestic domes of Vasily the Blessed cathedral, the restored Temple of Christ the Savior, New Maiden Convent, Don's and St. Daniel's monasteries, the palace-and-park ensembles of Kolomenskoe, Kuskovo and Ostankino.

Moscow is a cultural centre of global value. There are more than 70 theatres here, the best known of them the Bolshoi Theatre. Richest collections of painting, graphic art and sculpture are gathered in nearly hundred museums, among them the well-known Tretyakov picture gallery and the Museum of fine arts named after Pushkin. There are scores of concert halls, cinemas and expo-centers in the city.

Today's Moscow is a city of congresses, forums, festivals, industrial exhibitions and fairs, including the Moscow international film festival and the International tourist exhibition MITT.

A visit to the Russian capital gives lots of unforgettable and bright impressions to each and every tourist.

The environs of Moscow are also a whole world of cultural, historical and natural monuments. About 2200 tourist sights are officially registered and taken under protection by the state. The towns of Sergiev Posad, Zvenigorod (Ringing City), Serpukhov and Kolomna - situated near Moscow - attract more and more travelers every year.

Among the attractions of the Moscow area, a special place belongs to monasteries which for ages were spiritual centers of the country. The architectural complexes of Trinity-Sergiev's Lavra, New-Jerusalem or Joseph-Volokolamsk monasteries are of just unequalled beauty. And the manors situated near Moscow-Arkhangelskoye, Marphino, Abramtsevo, Sukhanovo, Melikhovo - are both picturesque and romantic.

The Golden Ring of Russia is the most popular tourist route which goes from Moscow to the northeast through old Russian towns: Sergiev Posad, Pereyaslavl-Zalessky, Rostov, Yaroslavl', Uglich, Kostroma, Suzdal', Vladimir and many other. There travelers will see scores of most interesting monuments of architecture and history of XII - XVII centuries.

Walls and towers of fortresses and monasteries, earthen banks, white-stone temples and masterpieces of wooden architecture, unique frescos and icons - all of these witnesses to the centuries passed preserve the unbreakable connection of the Golden Ring cities and allow one to see their common features, and to feel the soul of the ancient Rus'. The route around the Golden Ring involves some monuments of history and culture included in the UNESCO World Heritage List: the ensemble of Trinity-Sergiev's Lavra, the masterpieces of white-stone architecture in Vladimir and Suzdal'. The towns of the Golden Ring attract tourists with ancient Russian national crafts.

They are Rostov enamel and painted trays from Zhostovo, varnished caskets from Palekh and crystal wares of Gus'-Khrustalny (Goose-the-Crystal) glass-blowers. Traditions of ancient masters pass from generation to generation.

Everyone who loves Russian culture and art or interested in ancient Russian life should visit the Museum of wooden architecture and country life in Suzdal', the house-museum of artist Levitan in Plyos, and the museum Library of Russian Vodka in Uglich.

Historical and cultural monuments of the Vladimir region are incorporated into the tourist route Small Golden Ring. In addition to the cities of Vladimir and Suzdal', it includes other ancient Russian towns: Murom, Gus'-Khrustalny, Aleksandrov, Yuryev-Pol'sky, and Bogol'ubovo (God-loving) where at the confluence of the rivers the Nerl' and the Kl'az'ma - one of the most known monuments of old Russian stone architecture - the Church of Intercession on the Nerl' is situated.

Northern Palmira, Northern Venice, the City of White Nights... It has a lot of beautiful names, that majestic city of

Saint Petersburg, perhaps the most beautiful of all Russian cities! The Winter Palace, the spike of the Admiralty proudly shot up in the sky, the Spit of Vasilievsky island, St. Isaac and Kazan cathedrals, the Bronze Horseman, sculptures and most elegant railing of Letniy Sad (Summer Garden), canals and bridges on the Neva raised at night, treasures of the Hermitage and Russian Museum, Mariinsky Opera Theater, and unforgettable midnight sun - all these are features of the city. Saint Petersburg was the native place and cradle of Alexander Pushkin and Fyodor Dostoyevsky, Alexander Block and Anna Akhmatova. This city may be admired indefinitely!

The environs of Saint Petersburg are full of charm as well. You will never get tired of feasting your eyes upon the palaces and parks of Tsarskoe Selo, fountains of Peterhof, or alleys of Pavlovsk where well-known musical evenings were held, including concerts of "the King of Waltz" Johann Strauss.

The Silver Ring of Russia is the tourist route from Saint Petersburg through the northwest area, covering old Russian cities of Novgorod and Pskov, museum-reserve Pushkinskiye Gory (Pushkin Hills), and the cities of Ivangorod, Gdov and Porkhov with their ancient fortresses. Among historical and architectural monuments of this route a special place belongs to Novgorod Kremlin with its magnificent temples of XI - XV centuries.

The land of the Republic of Karelia to the north of Saint Petersburg is also rich in monuments of culture. The most important of them are the village of Kizhi - the largest in Russia architectural ensemble of national wooden architecture - and Valaam monastery, one of the spiritual centres of Russia established in XIV century on island Valaam in Ladoga lake.

Solovetskie islands with their Spaso-Preobrazhensky monastery having rich and complex history are often called a gem of the White Sea area and the pride of Russian North. Beautiful are the tourist centers in the north of Russia: the cities of Vologda, Arkhangelsk and Kargopol', and the well-known Kirillo-Belozersky Monastery where a most valuable collection of XV - XVIII centuries icons is kept.

The Volga-Mother, the great Russian river! It is a heroine of ancient legends (bylinas) and songs, an integral part of the image and spirit of Russia. Since olden days, the Volga was a major trading way. The cities founded on its banks, in different centuries, in due course have turned into large cultural centers of Russia.

Introduction to the Volga region frequently starts with Kostroma. This old Russian city, a gem of church architecture, is among the main tourist centers of the Golden Ring.

At the confluence of the Oka and Volga rivers, Nizhny Novgorod (Lower New-City) is located the largest Russian trading, scientific and cultural centre, a city with rich centuries-old history. The famous annual Nizhniy Novgorod Fair with its numerous exhibitions and forums is a specific feature of "Lower". The Nizhniy Novgorod land since long ago has been famous for its national crafts: Khokhloma and Gorodets lacquerware and Gorodets wood carving.

Another major city in the Volga region is Kazan', the capital of the Republic of Tatarstan. It has long and intricate history, and in its architectural monuments - such as Kazan Kremlin - primordially Russian spirit is fancifully bound with unique aroma of the East. Today Kazan is a large cultural center where Russian and Tatar national traditions coexist.

The image of the Middle Volga region is shaped by the old merchant cities of Samara, Saratov and Ulyanovsk (former Simbirsk). The largest cities of the southern Volga region are Volgograd and Astrakhan. Tsaritsyn-Stalingrad-Volgograd during its more than four-century history frequently found itself in the centre of the major events of the Russian social and state life. Quite remarkable is the architectural ensemble of Central Embankment of the city with its majestic memorial on Mamayev Kurgan in honor of Stalingrad defenders.

Italy Cultural Travel is a world leading provider of Independent Travel, Fully Escorted Tours, Small Group Tours and Private Luxury Tours experiences.

While our Fully Escorted Tours are for the Budget minded traveler, our Independent Travel, Small Group Tours and Private Luxury Tours are designed for discerning travelers seeking a more exclusive and personalised experience. Regardless of your budget, all of our Tours are fun and relaxing and provide a hands-on approach to discovering and experiencing history, culture and traditions.

While on our Fully Escorted Tours you will travel in a larger group which may vary from 30 to 50 other participants, on our Small Group Tours you will be in the company of only 10 to 20 other fellow travelers. In both circumstances you will still be provided with First Class Hotel accommodation which may vary from a minimum of 3 Star Superior to 4 Star Hotels.

On Small Group Tours you will travel beyond "tourist" hot spots and into the real lives, homes and workshops of our local friends and professionals. Experience gourmet indulgence, expert guided castle tours, vineyard walks and wine tasting tours, culinary classes and much more. Our Private Luxury Tours, combine: private transfers, custom designed excursions, activities not available to the general public, accommodations in deluxe and luxury historical hotels and gourmet dining with the company's favourite local Chefs.

China, Cultural Exchange, Educational Tourism, Technology, Free Speech and Internet Chat.

The flowery kingdom, now divided into China, Hong Kong and Taiwan, is having a difficult time managing the opportunities for dialogue available on the Web in internet chat rooms. The electronic exchange, combining as it does anonymity and directness, is confounding the social engineers of the three polities in distinctive but quite similar ways.

Nicholas Kristof in a New York Times Op Ed piece on December 13 reports on an experiment he attempted in Chinese internet chat rooms. Disguising himself as an ordinary individual and writing in Chinese he tried to post on several chat rooms the question "Why is Prime Minister Wen Jiabao off in America kowtowing to the imperialists when he should be solving more important problems at home." It did not get by the censors. A milder version was also censored but his third attempt was deemed acceptable by, as he put it, a cabianqui referring to the term for a ball that nicks the corner of the table in ping-pong. The third version was: "Prime Minister Wen Jiabao's visit to America has been very successful, but I wonder if he is wasting too much time abroad instead of focusing on our own important problems like unemployment?"

Similar efforts to nuance the politically acceptable in chat rooms is becoming an issue in Hong Kong. This report from Human Rights Watch discusses the problem. Just as with educational tourism and technology transfer there is in Internet chat rooms great potential for both great liberation and empowerment but simultaneously control and manipulation. One great paradox of technology is that it always presents itself in the guise of freedom, offering an easier and more effective life, but at the same time it enforces uniformity and compliance to external standards.

Kristof concludes his column noting that historically the Chinese would rebel when they had the chance and not necessarily when most oppressed. Thus we can anticipate, he believes , significant protest to come in China. Given the expansion of cultural exchange programs and educational tourism and the ease of communication made possible by technology a Tiananmen like violent repression is unlikely. But this is one reason why a "one China" policy is important despite the fact that political reunion between Taiwan and China is not going to happen. The point is to define a culturally Chinese form of freedom of expression, a form permitting cabianqiu but no more.

Whether you are looking for an affordable family holiday, a wine/culinary adventure, a cultural journey or a luxury experience, Italy Cultural Travel is the answer to all your travel needs.

Have you ever dreamed of staying in a Castle and waking up to the beauty of the Tuscan country side or staring away into the horizon while the sun is setting over Capri Island?

At the broadest level, the natural and cultural heritage belongs to all people. We each have a right and responsibility to understand, appreciate and conserve its universal values.

Heritage is a broad concept and includes the natural as well as the cultural environment. It encompasses landscapes, historic places, sites and built environments, as well as bio-diversity, collections, past and continuing cultural practices, knowledge and living experiences. It records and expresses the long processes of historic development, forming the essence of diverse national, regional, indigenous and local identities and is an integral part of modern life. It is a dynamic reference point and positive instrument for growth and change. The particular heritage and collective memory of each locality or community is irreplaceable and an important foundation for development, both now and into the future.

At a time of increasing globalisation, the protection, conservation, interpretation and presentation of the heritage and cultural diversity of any particular place or region is an important challenge for people everywhere. However, management of that heritage, within a framework of internationally recognised and appropriately applied standards, is usually the responsibility of the particular community or custodian group.

A primary objective for managing heritage is to communicate its significance and need for its conservation to its host community and to visitors. Reasonable and well managed physical, intellectual and/or emotive access to heritage and cultural development is both a right and a privilege. It brings with it a duty of respect for the heritage values, interests and equity of the present-day host community, indigenous custodians or owners of historic property and for the landscapes and cultures from which that heritage evolved.

The Dynamic Interaction between Tourism and Cultural Heritage

Domestic and international tourism continues to be among the foremost vehicles for cultural exchange, providing a personal experience, not only of that which has survived from the past, but of the contemporary life and society of others. It is increasingly appreciated as a positive force for natural and cultural conservation. Tourism can capture the economic characteristics of the heritage and harness these for conservation by generating funding, educating the community and influencing policy. It is an essential part of many national and regional economies and can be an important factor in development, when managed successfully.

Tourism itself has become an increasingly complex phenomenon, with political, economic, social, cultural, educational, bio-physical, ecological and aesthetic dimensions. The achievement of a beneficial inter-action between the potentially conflicting expectations and aspirations of visitors and host or local communities, presents many challenges and opportunities.

The natural and cultural heritage, diversities and living cultures are major tourism attractions. Excessive or poorly-managed tourism and tourism related development can threaten their physical nature, integrity and significant characteristics. The ecological setting, culture and lifestyles of host communities may also be degraded, along with the visitor's experience of the place.

Tourism should bring benefits to host communities and provide an important means and motivation for them to care for and maintain their heritage and cultural practices. The involvement and co-operation of local and/or indigenous community representatives, conservationists, tourism operators, property owners, policy makers, those preparing national development plans and site managers is necessary to achieve a sustainable tourism industry and enhance the protection of heritage resources for future generations.

ICOMOS, the International Council on Monuments and Sites, as the author of this Charter, other international organisations and the tourism industry, are dedicated to this challenge.

Objectives of the Charter

The Objectives of the International Cultural Tourism Charter are:

To facilitate and encourage those involved with heritage conservation and management to make the significance of that heritage accessible to the host community and visitors.

To facilitate and encourage the tourism industry to promote and manage tourism in ways that respect and enhance the heritage and living cultures of host communities.

To facilitate and encourage a dialogue between conservation interests and the tourism industry about the importance and fragile nature of heritage places, collections and living cultures, including the need to achieve a sustainable future for them.

To encourage those formulating plans and policies to develop detailed, measurable goals and strategies relating to the presentation and interpretation of heritage places and cultural activities, in the context of their preservation and conservation.

In Addition

The Charter supports wider initiatives by ICOMOS, other international bodies and the tourism industry in maintaining the integrity of heritage management and conservation.

The Charter encourages the involvement of all those with relevant or at times conflicting interests, responsibilities and obligations to join in achieving its objectives.

The Charter encourages the formulation of detailed guidelines by interested parties, facilitating the implementation of the Principles to their specific circumstances or the requirements of particular organisations and communities.

PRINCIPLES OF THE CULTURAL TOURISM CHARTER

Principle 1

Since domestic and international tourism is among the foremost vehicles for cultural exchange, conservation should provide responsible and well managed opportunities for members of the host community and visitors to experience and understand that community's heritage and culture at first hand.

1.1. The natural and cultural heritage is a material and spiritual resource, providing a narrative of historical development. It has an important role in modern life and should be made physically, intellectually and/or emotively accessible to the general public. Programmes for the protection and conservation of the physical attributes, intangible aspects, contemporary cultural expressions and broad context, should facilitate an understanding and appreciation of the heritage significance by the host community and the visitor, in an equitable and affordable manner.

1.2. Individual aspects of natural and cultural heritage have differing levels of significance, some with universal values, others of national, regional or local importance. Interpretation programmes should present that significance in a relevant and accessible manner to the host community and the visitor, with appropriate, stimulating and contemporary forms of education, media, technology and personal explanation of historical, environmental and cultural information.

1.3. Interpretation and presentation programmes should facilitate and encourage the high level of public awareness and support necessary for the long term survival of the natural and cultural heritage.

1.4. Interpretation programmes should present the significance of heritage places, traditions and cultural practices within the past experience and present diversities of the area and the host community, including that of minority cultural or linguistic groups. The visitor should always be informed of the differing cultural values that may be ascribed to a particular heritage resource.

Principle 2

The relationship between Heritage Places and Tourism is dynamic and may involve conflicting values. It should be managed in a sustainable way for present and future generations.

2.1. Places of heritage significance have an intrinsic value for all people as an important basis for cultural diversity and social development. The long term protection and conservation of living cultures, heritage places, collections,

then establish appropriate limits of acceptable c particularly in relation to the impact of visitor numbe the physical characteristics, integrity, ecology biodiversity of the place, local access and transportat systems and the social, economic and cultural well bein of the host community. If the likely level of change i unacceptable the development proposal should be modified.

2.7. There should be øn-going programmes of evaluation to assess the progressive impacts of tourism activities and development on the particular place or community.

Principle 3

Conservation and Tourism Planning for Heritage Places should ensure that the Visitor Experience will be worthwhile, satisfying and enjoyable.

3.1. Conservation and tourism programmes should present high quality information to optimise the visitor's understanding of the significant heritage characteristics and of the need for their protection, enabling the visitor to enjoy the place in an appropriate manner.

3.2. Visitors should be able to experience the heritage place at their own pace, if they so choose. Specific circulation routes may be necessary to minimise impacts on the integrity and physical fabric of a place, its natural and cultural characteristics.

3.3. Respect for the sanctity of spiritual places, practices and traditions is an important consideration for site managers, visitors, policy makers, planners and tourism operators. Visitors should be encouraged to behave as welcomed guests, respecting the values and lifestyles of the host community, rejecting possible theft or illicit trade in cultural property and conducting themselves in a responsible manner which would generate a renewed welcome, should they return.

3.4. Planning for tourism activities should provide appropriate facilities for the comfort, safety and well-being of the visitor, that enhance the enjoyment of the visit but do not adversely impact on the significant features or ecological characteristics.

Principle 4

Host communities and indigenous peoples should be involved in planning for conservation and tourism.

4.1. The rights and interests of the host community, at regional and local levels, property owners and relevant indigenous peoples who may exercise traditional rights or responsibilities over their own land and its significant sites, should be respected. They should be involved in establishing goals, strategies, policies and protocols for the identification, conservation, management, presentation and interpretation of their heritage resources, cultural practices and contemporary cultural expressions, in the tourism context.

4.2. While the heritage of any specific place or region may have a universal dimension, the needs and wishes of some communities or indigenous peoples to restrict or manage physical, spiritual or intellectual access to certain cultural practices, knowledge, beliefs, activities, artefacts or sites should be respected.

Principle 5

Tourism and conservation activities should benefit the host community.

5.1. Policy makers should promote measures for the equitable distribution of the benefits of tourism to be shared across countries or regions, improving the levels of socio-economic development and contributing where necessary to poverty alleviation.

5.2. Conservation management and tourism activities should provide equitable economic, social and cultural benefits to the men and women of the host or local community, at all levels, through education, training and the creation of full-time employment opportunities.

5.3. A significant proportion of the revenue specifically derived from tourism programmes to heritage places should be allotted to the protection, conservation and presentation of those places, including their natural and cultural contexts. Where possible, visitors should be advised of this revenue allocation.

5.4. Tourism programmes should encourage the training and employment of guides and site interpreters from the host community to enhance the skills of local people in the presentation and interpretation of their cultural values.

5.5. Heritage interpretation and education programmes among the people of the host community should encourage the involvement of local site interpreters. The programmes should promote a knowledge and respect for their heritage, encouraging the local people to take a direct interest in its care and conservation.

5.6. Conservation management and tourism programmes should include education and training opportunities for policy makers, planners, researchers, designers, architects, interpreters, conservators and tourism operators. Participants should be encouraged to understand and help resolve the at times conflicting issues, opportunities and problems encountered by their colleagues.

Principle 6

Tourism promotion programmes should protect and enhance Natural and Cultural Heritage characteristics.

6.1. Tourism promotion programmes should create realistic expectations and responsibly inform potential visitors of the specific heritage characteristics of a place or host community, thereby encouraging them to behave appropriately.

6.2. Places and collections of heritage significance should be promoted and managed in ways which protect their authenticity and enhance the visitor experience by minimising fluctuations in arrivals and avoiding excessive numbers of visitors at any one time.

6.3. Tourism promotion programmes should provide a wider distribution of benefits and relieve the pressures on more popular places by encouraging visitors to experience the wider cultural and natural heritage characteristics of the region or locality.

6.4. The promotion, distribution and sale of local crafts and other products should provide a reasonable social and economic return to the host community, while ensuring that their cultural integrity is not degraded.

Unesco

The United Nations Educational, Scientific and Cultural Organization (UNESCO is a specialized agency of the United Nations established on 16 November 1945. Its stated purpose is to contribute to peace and security by promoting international collaboration through education, science, and culture in order to further universal respect for justice, the rule of law, and the human rights along with fundamental freedoms proclaimed in the UN Charter. It is the heir of the League of Nations' International Commission on Intellectual Cooperation.

UNESCO has 193 Member States and seven Associate Members. The organization is based in Paris, France, with over 50 field offices and many specialized institutes and centres throughout the world. Most of the field offices are "cluster" offices covering three or more countries; there are also national and regional offices. UNESCO pursues its objectives through five major programs: education, natural sciences, social and human sciences, culture, and communication and information.

Projects sponsored by UNESCO include literacy, technical, and teacher-training programmes; international science programmes; the promotion of independent media and freedom of the press; regional and cultural history projects; the promotion of cultural diversity; international cooperation agreements to secure the world cultural and natural heritage (World Heritage Sites) and to preserve human rights, and attempts to bridge the worldwide digital divide.

MISSION AND PRIORITIES

UNESCO's mission is to contribute to the "building of peace", reducing the poverty, promoting sustainable development and intercultural dialogue through education, the sciences, culture, communication and information. The Organization focuses, in particular, on two global priorities: Africa and Gender Equality.

Other priorities of the Organization include attaining quality education for all and lifelong learning, addressing emerging social and ethical challenges, fostering cultural diversity, a culture of peace and building inclusive knowledge societies through information and communication.

The broad goals and concrete objectives of the international community - as set out in the internationally agreed development goals, including the Millennium Development Goals (MDGs) - underpin all UNESCO's strategies and activities.

History

UNESCO and its mandate for international intellectual co-operation can be traced back to the League of Nations resolution on 21 September 1921, to elect a Commission to study the question. The International Commission of Intellectual Co-operation (CICI) was officially created on 4

January 1922, as a consultative organ composed of individuals elected based on their personal qualifications.

The International Institute for Intellectual Cooperation (IICI) was then created in Paris on 9 August 1925, to act as the executing agency for the CICI. On 18 December 1925, the International Bureau of Education (IBE) began work as a non-governmental organization in the service of international educational development. However, the work of these predecessor organizations was largely interrupted by the onset of the Second World War.

After the signing of the Atlantic Charter and the Declaration of the United Nations, the Conference of Allied Ministers of Education (CAME) began meetings in London which continued between 16 November 1942 to 5 December 1945. On 30 October 1943, the necessity for an international organization was expressed in the Moscow Declaration, agreed upon by China, the United Kingdom, the United States of America and the USSR. This was followed by the Dumbarton Oaks Conference proposals of 9 October 1944.

Upon the proposal of CAME and in accordance with the recommendations of the United Nations Conference on International Organization (UNCIO), held in San Francisco in April-June 1945, a United Nations Conference for the establishment of an educational and cultural organization (ECO/CONF) was convened in London 1-16 November 1945. 44 governments were represented.

At the ECO/CONF, the Constitution of UNESCO was introduced and signed by 37 countries, and a Preparatory Commission was established. The Preparatory Commission operated between 16 November 1945, and 4 November 1946 - the date when UNESCO's Constitution came into force with the deposit of the twentieth ratification by a member state.

The first General Conference took place from 19 November to 10 December 1946, and elected Dr. Julian Huxley to the post of Director-General. The Constitution was amended in November 1954 when the General Conference resolved that members of the Executive Board would be representatives of the governments of the States of which they are nationals and would not, as before, act in their personal capacity.

This change in governance distinguished UNESCO from its predecessor, the CICI, in terms of how member states would work together in the Organization's fields of competence. As member states worked together over time to realize UNESCO's mandate, political and historical factors have shaped the Organization's operations in particular during the Cold War, the decolonization process, and the dissolution of the USSR.

Among the major achievements of the Organization is its work against racism, for example through influential statements on race starting with a declaration of anthropologists (among them was Claude Lévi-Strauss) and other scientists in 1950 and concluding with the 1978 Declaration on Race and Racial Prejudice. In 1956, the Republic of South Africa withdrew from UNESCO claiming that some of the Organization's publications amounted to "interference" in the country's "racial problems." South Africa rejoined the Organization in 1994 under the leadership of Nelson Mandela.

UNESCO's early work in the field of education included the pilot project on fundamental education in the Marbial Valley, Haiti, started in 1947. This project was followed by expert missions to other countries, including, for example, a mission to Afghanistan in 1949. In 1948, UNESCO recommended that Member States should make free primary education compulsory and universal. In 1990 the World Conference on Education for All, in Jomtien, Thailand, launched a global movement to provide basic education for all children, youths and adults.

Ten years later, the 2000 World Education Forum held in Dakar, Senegal, led member governments to commit to achieving basic education for all by 2015.

UNESCO's early activities in the field of culture included, for example, the Nubia Campaign, launched in 1960. The purpose of the campaign was to move the Great Temple of Abu Simbel to keep it from being swamped by the Nile after construction of the Aswan Dam. During the 20-year campaign, 22 monuments and architectural complexes were relocated. This was the first and largest in a series of campaigns including Moenjodaro (Pakistan), Fez (Morocco), Kathmandu (Nepal), Borobudur (Indonesia) and the Acropolis (Greece).

The Organization's work on heritage led to the adoption, in 1972, of the Convention concerning the Protection of the World Cultural and Natural Heritage. The World Heritage Committee was established in 1976 and the first sites inscribed on the World Heritage List in 1978. Since then important legal instruments on cultural heritage and diversity have been adopted by UNESCO member states in 2003 (Convention for the Safeguarding of the Intangible Cultural Heritage) and 2005 (Convention on the Protection and Promotion of the Diversity of Cultural Expressions).

At an intergovernmental meeting of UNESCO in Paris in December 1951 was held which led to the creation of the European Council for Nuclear Research (CERN) in 1954. The World Wide Web was born at CERN in 1989.

Arid Zone programming, 1948-1966, is another example of an early major UNESCO project in the field of natural sciences. In 1968, UNESCO organized the first intergovernmental conference aimed at reconciling the environment and development, a problem which continues to be addressed in the field of sustainable development. The main outcome of the 1968 conference was the creation of UNESCO's Man and the Biosphere Programme.

In the field of communication, the free flow of information has been a priority for UNESCO from its beginnings. In the years immediately following World War

II, efforts were concentrated on reconstruction and on the identification of needs for means of mass communication around the world. UNESCO started organizing training and education for journalists in the 1950s.

In response to calls for a "New World Information and Communication Order" in the late 1970s, UNESCO established the International Commission for the Study of Communication Problems, which produced the 1980 MacBride report (named after the Chair of the Commission, the Nobel Peace Prize laureate Seán MacBride). Following the MacBride report, UNESCO introduced the Information Society for All programme and Toward Knowledge Societies programme in the lead up to the World Summit on the Information Society in 2003 (Geneva) and 2005 (Tunis).

Activities

UNESCO implements its activities through the five programme areas of Education, Natural Sciences, Social and Human Sciences, Culture, and Communication and Information.

- Education: UNESCO is providing international leadership in creating learning societies with educational opportunities for all; it supports research in Comparative education; and provides expertise and fosters partnerships to strengthen national educational leadership and the capacity of countries to offer quality education for all. This includes the
    - Eight specialized Institutes in different topics of the sector
    - UNESCO Chairs, an international network of 644 UNESCO Chairs, involving over 770 institutions in 126 countries.
    - Environmental Conservation Organisation

- o Organization of the International Conference on Adult Education (CONFINTEA) in an interval of 12 years
- o UNESCO ASPNet, an international network of 8,000 schools in 170 countries

UNESCO does not accredit institutions of higher learning.

- UNESCO also issues public 'statements' to educate the public:
    - o Seville Statement on Violence: A statement adopted by UNESCO in 1989 to refute the notion that humans are biologically predisposed to organised violence.
- Designating projects and places of cultural and scientific significance, such as:
    - o International Network of Geoparks
    - o Biosphere reserves, through the Programme on Man and the Biosphere (MAB), since 1971
    - o City of Literature; in 2007, the first city to be given this title was Edinburgh, the site of Scotland's first circulating library. In 2008, Iowa City, Iowa became the City of Literature.
    - o Endangered languages and linguistic diversity projects
    - o Masterpieces of the Oral and Intangible Heritage of Humanity
    - o Memory of the World International Register, since 1997
    - o Water resources management, through the International Hydrological Programme (IHP), since 1965
    - o World Heritage Sites

- Encouraging the "free flow of ideas by images and words" by:
  - o Promoting freedom of expression, press freedom and access to information, through the International Programme for the Development of Communication and the Communication and Information Programme
  - o Promoting universal access to ICTs, through the Information for All Programme (IFAP)
  - o Promoting Pluralism and cultural diversity in the media
- Promoting events, such as:
  - o International Decade for the Promotion of a Culture of Peace and Non-Violence for the Children of the World: 2001-2010, proclaimed by the UN in 1998
  - o World Press Freedom Day, 3 May each year, to promote freedom of expression and freedom of the press as a basic human right and as crucial components of any healthy, democratic and free society.
  - o Criança Esperança in Brazil, in partnership with Rede Globo, to raise funds for community-based projects that foster social integration and violence prevention.
  - o International Literacy Day
  - o International Year for the Culture of Peace
- Founding and funding projects, such as:
  - o Migration Museums Initiative: Promoting the establishment of museums for cultural dialogue with migrant populations.
  - o UNESCO-CEPES, the European Centre for Higher Education: established in 1972 in

Bucharest, Romania, as a de-centralized office to promote international co-operation in higher education in Europe as well as Canada, USA and Israel. Higher Education in Europe is its official journal.

- Free Software Directory: since 1998 UNESCO and the Free Software Foundation have jointly funded this project cataloguing free software.
- FRESH Focussing Resources on Effective School Health.
- OANA, the Organization of Asia-Pacific News Agencies
- International Council of Science
- UNESCO Goodwill Ambassadors
- ASOMPS, Asian Symposium on Medicinal Plants and Spices, a series of scientific conferences held in Asia
- Botany 2000, a programme supporting taxonomy, and biological and cultural diversity of medicinal and ornamental plants, and their protection against environmental pollution

Official UNESCO NGOs

UNESCO enjoys official relations with 322 international NGOs. Most of these are what UNESCO calls "operational", a select few are "formal". Operational relations are reserved for an NGO with an active presence in the field, with special expertise and with an ability to channel the concerns of their clients. Requests for admission by an NGO to UNESCO for operational relations can be made to the Director-General at any time. Formal relations are reserved for those NGOs who have a sustained role in cooperating with UNESCO both upstream and downstream.

Admission for formal recognition is only granted to international NGOs that are widely representative and expert in their field of activity, and with a genuinely international structure and membership. Formal relations are themselves sub-divided into two types, "consultative" or "associate", depending on the role and structure of the NGO itself. The Executive Board, one of UNESCO's governing bodies, decides on requests for admission by NGOs to one or the other type of formal relation on the basis of recommendations made by the Director-General. Formal relations are established for renewable periods of six years.

The highest form of affiliation to UNESCO is "formal associate", and the 22 NGOs with formal associate (ASC) relations occupying offices at UNESCO are:

1. International Baccalaureate (IB)
2. Coordinating Committee for International Voluntary Service (CCIVS)
3. Education International (EI)
4. International Association of Universities (IAU)
5. International Council for Film, Television and Audiovisual Communication (IFTC)
6. International Council for Philosophy and Humanistic Studies (ICPHS) which publishes Diogenes
7. International Council for Science (ICSU)
8. International Council of Museums (ICOM)
9. International Council of Sport Science and Physical Education (ICSSPE)
10. International Council on Archives (ICA)
11. International Council on Monuments and Sites (ICOMOS)
12. International Federation of Journalists (IFJ)

13. International Federation of Library Associations and Institutions (IFLA)
14. International Federation of Poetry Associations (IFPA)
15. International Music Council (IMC)
16. International Scientific Council for Island Development (INSULA)
17. International Social Science Council (ISSC)
18. International Theatre Institute (ITI)
19. International Union for Conservation of Nature and Natural Resources (IUCN)
20. International Union of Technical Associations and Organizations
21. Union of International Associations (UIA)
22. World Association of Newspapers (WAN)
23. World Federation of Engineering Organizations (WFEO)
24. World Federation of UNESCO Clubs, Centres and Associations (WFUCA)

UNESCO Institutes and Centres

The institutes are specialized departments of the Organization that support UNESCO's programme, providing specialized support for cluster and national offices.

Education

- UNESCO International Bureau of Education (IBE); Geneva (Switzerland) specializes in educational contents, methods and structures. IBE shares expertise on curriculum development and aims to introduce innovative approaches in curriculum design and implementation, improve practical skills, and facilitate international dialogue on educational policies and practices.

- UNESCO Institute for Lifelong Learning promotes lifelong learning policy and practice with a focus on adult learning and education, especially literacy and non-formal education and alternative learning opportunities for marginalized and disadvantaged groups.
- UNESCO International Institute for Educational Planning (IIEP); Paris (France) and Buenos Aires (Argentina) is a centre for training and research to strengthen the capacity of countries to plan and manage their education systems.
- UNESCO Institute for Information Technologies in Education (IITE); Moscow (Russian Federation) serves as a centre of excellence and provider of technical support and expertise in the area of ICT usage in education.
- UNESCO International Institute for Capacity-Building in Africa (IICBA); Addis Ababa (Ethiopia) works to enhance the capacities of regional, national and local level educational institutions in Africa, thus providing the opportunity for technological improvements, such as the utilization of electronic media for networking and for educational purposes, targeting both individuals and institutions.
- UNESCO International Institute for Higher Education in Latin America and the Caribbean (IESALC); Caracas (Venezuela) contributes to the development and transformation of the tertiary education through the reinforcement of a work plan that, among other purposes, attempts to be an instrument to support the management of change and the required transformations in order that

higher education in the region becomes an effective promoter of a culture of peace that allows to make viable - in an age of globalization - the human sustainable development based on principles of justice, equity, freedom, solidarity, democracy and respect of the human rights.

- UNESCO International Centre for Technical and Vocational Education and Training (UNEVOC); Bonn (Germany) works to strengthen and upgrade countries' Technical and Vocational Education and Training (TVET) systems.
- UNESCO European Centre for Higher Education (CEPES); Bucarest (Romania) promotes co-operation and provides technical support in the field of higher education among UNESCO's Member States in Central, Eastern and South-East Europe.

Natural Sciences

- UNESCO Institute for Water Education (IHE); Delft (Netherlands)the largest water education facility in the world, and the only institution in the UN system authorised to confer accredited MSc degrees.
- International Centre for Theoretical Physics (ICTP); Trieste (Italy) aims to foster growth of advanced studies and research in physical and mathematical sciences, develops high level programmes and conducts research especially in developing countries.

Statistics

- UNESCO Institute for Statistics (UIS); Montreal (Canada) provides an impressive collection of up to date statistics in the fields of education, science and technology, culture and communication.

Official list of UNESCO Prizes

UNESCO currently awards 22 prizes in education, science, culture and peace:

- Félix Houphouët-Boigny Peace Prize
- L'Oréal-UNESCO Awards for Women in Science
- UNESCO/King Sejong Literacy Prize
- UNESCO/Confucius Prize for Literacy
- UNESCO/Emir Jaber al-Ahmad al-Jaber al-Sabah Prize to promote Quality Education for Persons with Intellectual Disabilities
- UNESCO King Hamad Bin Isa Al-Khalifa Prize for the Use of Information and Communication Technologies in Education
- UNESCO/Hamdan Bin Rashid Al-Maktoum Prize for Outstanding Practice and Performance in Enhancing the Effectiveness of Teachers
- UNESCO/Kalinga Prize for the Popularization of Science
- UNESCO/Institut Pasteur Medal for an outstanding contribution to the development of scientific knowledge that has a beneficial impact on human health
- UNESCO/Sultan Qaboos Prize for Environmental Preservation
- Great Man-Made River International Water Prize for Water Resources in Arid Zones presented by UNESCO (title to be reconsidered)
- Michel Batisse Award for Biosphere Reserve Management
- UNESCO/Obiang Nguema Mbasogo International Prize for Research in the Life Sciences

- UNESCO/Bilbao Prize for the Promotion of a Culture of Human Rights
- UNESCO Prize for Peace Education
- UNESCO-Madanjeet Singh Prize for the Promotion of Tolerance and Non-Violence
- UNESCO/International José Martí Prize
- UNESCO/Avicenna Prize for Ethics in Science
- UNESCO/Juan Bosch Prize for the Promotion of Social Science Research in Latin America and the Caribbean
- Sharjah Prize for Arab Culture
- Melina Mercouri International Prize for the Safeguarding and Management of Cultural Landscapes (UNESCO-Greece)
- IPDC-UNESCO Prize for Rural Communication
- UNESCO/Guillermo Cano World Press Freedom Prize
- UNESCO/Jikji Memory of the World Prize

Member States

As of October 2009, UNESCO counts 193 Member States and seven Associate Members. Some member states have additional National Organizing Committees from some of their dependent territories.

Postage Stamps

Various countries have issued postage stamps commemorating UNESCO. The organization's seal and its headquarters building have been common themes. In 1955 the United Nations Postal Administration (UNPA) issued its first ones honouring the organization.

While UNESCO has never separately issued stamps valid for postage, from 1951 to 1966 it issued a series of 41 "gift stamps" to raise money for its activities. Designed by artists in various countries, they were sold at a desk by the UNPA counter located in the United Nations Headquarters building in New York City. No longer available at the UN, most of these Cinderella stamps can be purchased at low cost from speciality stamp dealers.

Directors-General

1. Julian Huxley (1946-1948)
2. Jaime Torres Bodet (1948-1952)
3. John Wilkinson Taylor (acting 1952-1953)
4. Luther Evans (1953-1958)
5. Vittorino Veronese (1958-1961)
6. René Maheu (1961-1974; acting 1961)
7. Amadou-Mahtar M'Bow (1974-1987)
8. Federico Mayor Zaragoza (1987-1999)
9. Koïchiro Matsuura (1999-2009)
10. Irina Bokova (2009-)

UNESCO Offices

Through its field offices, UNESCO develops strategies, programmes and activities in consultation with national authorities and other partners.

Office Kypes

UNESCO's field offices are categorized into four primary office types based upon their function and geographic coverage. The following descriptions identify the primary dividing lines.

Cluster Offices

A cluster office covers a group of countries and is the central component in the field, around which are organized national offices and regional bureaux. The 27 cluster offices, covering 148 Member States, represent the main supporting structure of UNESCO Secretariat's network in the field.

National Offices

In addition to cluster offices which are the main supporting structure of the Secretariat's network in the field, there are 21 national offices, each serving a single Member State. These exceptions to the cluster system involve either the so-called E-9 countries (nine highly-populated countries) which are either in post-conflict situations or are in transition.

Regional Sureaux

Regional bureaux and regional advisers specializing in the fields of education, science, the social sciences, culture and communication provide specialized support to cluster and national offices in a given region.

Liaison Offices

The decentralized network includes two liaison offices to the United Nations in New York and Geneva and a liaison office to the European Union in Brussels.

UNESCO Field Offices by Region

The following list of all UNESCO Field Offices is organized geographically by UNESCO Region and identifies the members states and associate members of UNESCO which are served by each office.

Africa

UNESCO Office in Harare Headquarters

- Abuja - National Office to Nigeria.
- Accra - Cluster Office for Benin, Côte d'Ivoire, Ghana, Liberia, Nigeria, Sierra Leone and Togo.

- Addis Ababa - Cluster Office for Djibouti and Ethiopia.
- Bamako - Cluster Office for Burkina Faso, Guinea, Mali and Niger.
- Brazzaville - National Office to Congo.
- Bujumbura - National Office to Burundi.
- Dakar - Regional Bureau for Education in Africa and Cluster Office for Cape Verde, Gambia, Guinea-Bissau, and Senegal.
- Dar es-Salaam - Cluster Office for Comoros, Madagascar, Mauritius, Seychelles and United Republic of Tanzania.
- Harare - Cluster Office for Botswana, Malawi, Mozambique, Zambia, and Zimbabwe.
- Kinshasa - National Office to the Democratic Republic of Congo.
- Libreville - Cluster Office for Democratic Republic of the Congo, Equatorial Guinea, Gabon, Sao Tome and Principe.
- Maputo - National Office to Mozambique.
- Nairobi - Regional Bureau for Sciences in Africa and Cluster Office for Burundi, Eritrea, Kenya, Rwanda, Somalia and Uganda.
- Windhoek - Cluster Office to Angola, Lesotho, Namibia, South Africa and Swaziland.
- Yaoundé - Cluster Office to Cameroon, Central African Republic and Chad.

Arab States

UNESCO Office for Iraq Headquarters

- Iraq - National Office for Iraq.
- Amman - National Office to Jordan.

- Beirut - Regional Bureau for Education in the Arab States and Cluster Office to Lebanon, Syria, Jordan, Iraq and the Autonomous Palestinian Territories.
- Cairo - Regional Bureau for Sciences in the Arab States and Cluster Office for Egypt, Libyan Arab Jamahiriya and Sudan.
- Doha - Cluster Office to Bahrain, Kuwait, Oman, Qatar, Saudi Arabia, United Arab Emirates and Yemen.
- Khartoum - National Office to Sudan.
- Rabat - Cluster Office to Algeria, Mauritania, Morocco and Tunisia.
- Ramallah - National Office to the Palestinian Authority.

Asia and Pacific

- Almaty - Cluster Office to Kazakhstan, Kyrgyzstan, Tajikistan and Uzbekistan.
- Apia - Cluster Office to Australia, Cook Islands, Fiji, Kiribati, Marshall Islands, Micronesia (Federated States of), Nauru, New Zealand, Niue, Palau, Papua New Guinea, Samoa, Solomon Islands, Tonga, Tuvalu, Vanuatu and Tokelau (Associate Member).
- Bangkok - Regional Bureau for Education in Asia and the Pacific and Cluster Office to Thailand, Myanmar, Lao PDR, Singapore, Viet Nam and Cambodia.
- Beijing - Cluster Office to the Democratic People's Republic of Korea (DPRK), Japan, Mongolia, the People's Republic of China and the Republic of Korea (ROK).
- Dhaka - National Office to Bangladesh.
- Hanoi - National Office to Vietnam.

- Islamabad - National Office to Pakistan.
- Jakarta - Regional Bureau for Sciences in Asia and the Pacific and Cluster Office to Brunei Darussalam, Indonesia, Malaysia, the Philippines, and Timor Leste.
- Kabul - National Office to Afghanistan.
- Kathmandu - National Office to Nepal.
- New Delhi - Cluster Office to Bangladesh, Bhutan, India, Maldives, Nepal and Sri Lanka.
- Phnom Penh - National Office to Cambodia.
- Tashkent - National Office to Uzbekistan.
- Tehran - Cluster Office to the Islamic Republic of Afghanistan, the Islamic Republic of Iran, the Islamic Republic of Pakistan and Turkmenistan.

Europe and North America

- Brussels - Liaison Office to the European Union and its subsidiary bodies in Brussels.
- Geneva - Liaison Office to the United Nations in Geneva.
- New York - Liaison Office to the United Nations in New York.
- Moscow - Cluster Office to Armenia, Azerbaijan, Belarus, Republic of Moldova and the Russian Federation.
- Venice - UNESCO Venice Office Regional Bureau for Science and Culture in Europe.

Latin America and the Caribbean

UNESCO Office in San José Headquarters

- Brasilia - National Office to Brazil.
- Guatemala - National Office to Guatemala.

- Havana - Regional Bureau for Culture in Latin America and the Caribbean and Cluster Office to Cuba, Dominican Republic, Haiti and Aruba.
- Kingston - Cluster Office to Antigua and Barbuda, Bahamas, Barbados, Belize, Dominica, Grenada, Guyana, Jamaica, Saint Kitts and Nevis, Saint Lucia, Saint Vincent and the Grenadines, Suriname and Trinidad and Tobago as well as the associate member states of British Virgin Islands, Netherlands Antilles and Cayman Islands.
- Lima - National Office to Peru.
- Mexico - National Office to Mexico.
- Montevideo - Regional Bureau for Sciences in Latin America and the Caribbean and Cluster Office to Argentina, Brazil, Chile, Paraguay and Uruguay.
- Port-au-Prince - National Office to Haiti.
- Quito - Cluster Office to Bolivia, Colombia, Ecuador and Venezuela.
- San José - Cluster Office to Costa Rica, El Salvador, Guatemala, Honduras, Mexico, Nicaragua and Panama.
- Santiago de Chile - Regional Bureau for Education in Latin America and the Caribbean and National Office to Chile.

Elections

Elections for the renewal of the position of Director-General took place in Paris from 7 September to 23 September 2009. Eight candidates ran for the position, and 58 countries voted for them. The Executive Council gathered from 7 September to 23 September, the vote itself beginning on the 17th. Irina Bokova was elected the new Director-General.

CONTROVERSY AND REFORM

New World Information and Communication Order

UNESCO has been the center of controversy in the past, particularly in its relationships with the United States, the United Kingdom, Singapore, and the former Soviet Union. During the 1970s and 1980s, UNESCO's support for a "New World Information and Communication Order" and its MacBride report calling for democratization of the media and more egalitarian access to information was condemned in these countries as attempts to curb freedom of the press.

UNESCO was perceived by some as a platform for communists and Third World dictators to attack the West, a stark contrast to accusations made by the USSR in the late 1940s and early 1950s. In 1984, the United States withheld its contributions and withdrew from the organization in protest, followed by the United Kingdom in 1985 and Singapore in 1986. Following a change of government in 1997, the UK rejoined. The United States rejoined in 2003, followed by Singapore on 8 October 2007.

Internal Reforms

Part of the reason for their change of stance was due to considerable reforms implemented by UNESCO over the past 10 years. These included the following measures: the number of divisions in UNESCO was cut in half, allowing a corresponding halving of the number of Directors-from 200 to under 100, out of a total staff of approximately 2,000 worldwide. At the same time, the number of field units was cut from a peak of 1,287 in 1998 to 93 today. Parallel management structures, including 35 Cabinet-level special adviser positions, were abolished.

Between 1998 and 2009, 245 negotiated staff departures and buy-outs took place, causing the inherited $12 million staff cost deficit to disappear. The staff pyramid, which was the most top-heavy in the UN system, was cut back as the number of high-level posts was halved and the "inflation" of posts was reversed through the down-grading of many positions.

Open competitive recruitment, results-based appraisal of staff, training of all managers and field rotation were instituted, as well as SISTER and SAP systems for transparency in results-based programming and budgeting. In addition, the Internal Oversight Service (IOS) was established in 2001 to improve organizational performance by including the lessons learned from programme evaluations into the overall reform process. It regularly carries out audits of UNESCO offices that essentially look into administrative and procedural compliance, but do not assess the relevance and usefulness of the activities and projects that are carried out. At least in thoery, the evaluation of the relevance and effectiveness of programmes is carried out by the Evaluation Section of IOS, although evidence of using "lessons learned" in programming is less clear and not always free from donor preferences.

Israel

In October 2010, UNESCO's Executive Board voted to include Rachel's Tomb in Bethlehem on the West Bank referring to it as the 'Bilal Bin Rabah Mosque/Rachel's Tomb and a part of Palestinian territory under occupation. The board demanded that Israel remove the site from its own list of National Heritage Sites, even though the site has had Jewish significance for thousands of years, on the grounds that this unilateral action was a violation of international law.

Subsequently, Israel partially suspended ties with UNESCO. Danny Ayalon, the Deputy Foreign Minister of Israel, declared that it was another example of campaign of delegitimization that the Palestinian National Authority was waging and that it hurt UNESCO for seeming to be a rubber stamp. Zevulun Orlev, chairman of Israel's Education and Culture Committee, referred to the resolutions as an attempt undermine the mission of UNESCO as a scientific and cultural organization that promotes cooperation throughout the world.

CHAPTER–8

ADULT AND SENIORS' EDUCATIONAL TOURISM

Adult education is the practice of teaching and educating adults. Adult education takes place in the workplace, through 'extension' school (e.g. Harvard Extension) or 'school of continuing education' or 'school of general studies' (Columbia General Studies). Other learning places include folk high schools, community colleges, and lifelong learning centers. The practice is also often referred to as 'Training and Development 'and is often associated with workforce or professional development. Adult education is different from vocational education, which is mostly workplace-based for skill improvement; and also from non-formal adult education, including learning skills or learning for personal development.

There are many opportunities to participate in adult education programmes in Andalucía. To a certain extent your options will depend on your language skills.

IF YOU SPEAK SOME SPANISH

Local governments typically sponsor a wide variety of educational activities for all ages. To find these programmes, simply visit the Town Hall in the area where you are staying and you will be directed to the appropriate centre.

If you are hoping to learn to paint, make yourself a new set of ceramic dishes, weave in traditional Spanish fashion or dance flamenco you will probably be sent to the municipally-sponsored Casa de Cultura - or culture house. Even if you are only going to be here for a few weeks or months you might be lucky enough to get into one of these very inexpensive courses, that are open to anyone interested in joining, provided there is space available.

Music courses are inexpensive at public conservatories, but designed specifically for children and young adults. Therefore, if you are interested in studying music in any form, the conservatory will interest you more as an excellent place to find a private teacher either through posted advertisements or by asking the administration for a recommendation.

Should you be looking to pursue more athletic interests, you will very likely head in the direction of the town's "polideportivo" or municipally sponsored sports section. Here everything from water aerobics, regular aerobics, tai chi, weight training and educational nature walks might be on the agenda. Classes vary greatly from centre to centre, so it is often worthwhile to shop around.

Spanish universities also accept "mature students" and international programmes offering a variety of business, language, culture and history courses also operate on all major Andalusian university campuses.

Finally, another source of ongoing education can be found by combing the classifieds in the local, English language press. It is not difficult to find private teachers for music, computer and language courses. A large variety of clubs and associations also operate and some, such as the music appreciation association, serve educational as well as social aims.

FOR NON-SPANISH SPEAKERS

If you don't speak Spanish and you are wishing to pursue adult education opportunities during your stay in Andalucía, you could either immerse yourself in the culture while you're here, sign up for intensive language courses, or get in touch with the local branch of the U3A, or University of the Third Age. This intriguing, not-for-profit organisation depends on members - mostly retired - to share professional knowledge and skills with each other in organised courses. At the time of writing (2003) the U3A only operates in Andalucía on the Costa del Sol, but it is a very active group and might offer anything from photography (a wonderful way to get to know this area better while you are on holiday), Spanish culture, history, language and literature courses. To learn more, send an e-mail to the U3A, Costa del Sol's president, Carmella Dight at carmella@ya.com.

Programs provide one to one tutoring and small group sessions for adults at the 6th grade level or below. Public libraries, nonprofit organizations and school systems administer these programs across the country. Many adult education centers from community colleges receive grants from Welfare and Unemployment departments to offer training to welfare and unemployment recipients to help these individuals gain life and work skills to facilitate their return to the mainstream. They also provide programs for ex-offenders to reintegrate to society.

Educating adults differs from educating children in several ways. One of the most important differences is that adults have accumulated knowledge, work experience or military service that can add to the learning experience. Another difference is that most adult education is voluntary, therefore, the participants are generally better motivated.

Adults frequently apply their knowledge in a practical fashion to learn effectively. They must have a reasonable expectation that the knowledge recently gained will help them further their goals. One example, common in the 1990s, was the proliferation of computer training courses in which adults (not children or adolescents), most of whom were office workers, could enroll. These courses would teach basic use of the operating system or specific application software. Because the abstractions governing the user's interactions with a PC were so new, many people who had been working white-collar jobs for ten years or more eventually took such training courses, either at their own whim (to gain computer skills and thus earn higher pay) or at the behest of their managers.

In the United States, a more general example, and stereotypical,is that of the high-school dropout who returns to school to complete general education requirements. Most upwardly-mobile positions require at the very least a high school diploma or equivalent. A working adult is unlikely to have the freedom to simply quit his or her job and go "back to school" full time. Public school systems and community colleges usually offer evening or weekend classes for this reason. In Europe this is often referred to as "second-chance", and many schools offer tailor-made courses and learning programs for these returning learners.

Those adults who read at the very lowest level get help from volunteer literacy programs. These national organizations provide training, tutor certification, and accreditation for local volunteer programs. States often have state organizations such as Literacy Florida!Inc., which provide field services for volunteer literacy programs.

In the U.S.A., the equivalent of the high school diploma earned by an adult through these programs is to pass the General Education Development (GED) test.

Another fast-growing sector of adult education is English for Speakers of Other Languages (ESOL), also referred to as English as a Second Language (ESL) or English Language Learners (ELL). These courses are key in assisting immigrants with not only the acquisition of the English language, but the acclimation process to the culture of the United States.

A common problem in adult education in the U.S. is the lack of professional development opportunities for adult educators. Most adult educators come from other professions and are not well trained to deal with adult learning issues. Most of the positions available in this field are only part-time without any benefits or stability since they are usually funded by government grants that might last for only a couple of years. These educators face many difficulties at professional and personal levels and are rarely equipped to empower their adult learners.

COMMUNITY COLLEGE

A community college is a type of educational institution. The term can have different meanings in different countries.

Australia

Australia has had a system of Technical and Further Education (TAFE) and Community Colleges for many years. Training is conducted under the National Training System, the Australian system for vocational education and training (VET) under the Australian Quality Training Framework (AQTF), in which employers, the States of Australia, and the Commonwealth Government, formalise a curriculum available for Registered Training Organisations (RTOs) to teach and assess the competency of students. Courses are part of the Australian Qualifications Framework.

TAFEs or their outlying schools are in most large towns, and cities.

Community Colleges Australia provide affordable education, training & lifestyle courses to their local communities. There are over 50 Community Colleges across New South Wales and Victoria. SGSCC - St George & Sutherland Community College is one of the largest colleges with a 30 year history, the college specialises in Disability, Leisure, Work Skills, School Age and English programs.

Canada

In Canada, the 150 institutions that are the rough equivalent of the US community college are usually referred to as "colleges" since in common usage a degree granting institution is almost exclusively a university. In the province of Quebec, even when speaking in English, colleges are called Cégeps for Collège d'enseignement général et professionnel, meaning "College of General and Vocational Education". (The word College can also refer to a private High School in Quebec). Colleges are educational institution providing higher education and tertiary education, granting certificates, diplomas, associate's degrees, and bachelor's degrees. Each Province has its own system of Colleges reflecting the decentralization of the Canadian Education system as provided for in The Constitution Act, 1867.

However virtually all of them began in the mid 1960's as a response to the shortage of skilled immigrants as the wave of post second World War II Europeans began to decline just as the Canadian economy was beginning to expand rapidly. The motivation was economic as opposed to the much earlier start in the United States of Junior and Community Colleges which was driven by an integrative social policy.

Canadian Community College Systems

- Nova Scotia Community College system
- Ontario Colleges
- Quebec CEGEPs
- New Brunswick Community College

Malaysia

Community colleges in Malaysia are a network of educational institutions whereby vocational and technical skills training could be provided at all levels for school leavers before they entered the workforce. The community colleges also provide an infrastructure for rural communities to gain skills training through short courses as well as providing access to a post-secondary education.

At the moment, most community colleges award qualifications up to Level 3 in the Malaysian Qualifications Framework (Certificate 3) in both the Skills sector (Sijil Kemahiran Malaysia or the Malaysian Skills Certificate) as well as the Vocational and Training sector but the number of community colleges that are starting to award Level 4 qualifications (Diploma) are increasing.

This is two levels below a Bachelor's degree (Level 6 in the MQF) and students within the system who intend to further their studies to that level will usually seek entry into Advanced Diploma programs in public universities, polytechnics or accredited private providers.

Philippines

In the Philippines, a community school functions as elementary or secondary school at daytime and towards the end of the day convert into a community college. This type of institution offers night classes under the supervision of the same principal, and the same faculty members who are given part time college teaching load.

The concept of community college dates back to the time of the former Minister of Education, Culture and Sports (MECS) that had under its wings the Bureaus of Elementary Education, Secondary Education, Higher Education and Vocational-Technical Education. MECS Secretary, Dr. Cecilio Putong, who in 1971 wrote that a community school is a school established in the community, by the community, and for the community itself. Dr. Pedro T. Orata of Pangasinan shared the same idea, hence the establishment of a Community College, now called the City College of Urdaneta.

A community college like the one in Abuyog, Leyte can operate with only PHP 124,000 annual budget in a 2-storey structure housing more than 700 students.

United Kingdom

In the United Kingdom, 'community' college usually refers to Sixth Form in Secondary School, College or post compulsory education institution and is where students can achieve the A-levels, Scottish Higher, or other vocational qualifications (such as a GNVQ or an HND for example) needed for University. In other cases Community Colleges can also provide GCSEs to students of Compulsory School ages.

United States

In the United States, community colleges, sometimes called junior colleges, technical colleges, or city colleges, are primarily two-year public institutions providing higher education and lower-level tertiary education, granting certificates, diplomas, and associate's degrees.

After graduating from a community college, some students transfer to a four-year liberal arts college or university for two to three years to complete a bachelor's degree.

Before the 1970s, community colleges in the United States were more commonly referred to as junior colleges, and that term is still used at some institutions. However, the term "junior college" has evolved to describe private two-year institutions, whereas the term "community college" has evolved to describe publicly funded two-year institutions. The name derives from the fact that community colleges primarily attract and accept students from the local community, and are often supported by local tax revenue.

Comprehensive Community Colleges

Many schools have evolved into and adapted the term Comprehensive to describe their institutions. These schools typically offer five facets of education.

- Transfer Education - The traditional two-year student that will then transfer to a four-year institution to pursue a BS/BA degree.
- Career Education - The traditional two-year student that will graduate with an Associate Degree and directly enter the workforce.
- Developmental - Remedial education for high school graduates who are not academically ready to enroll in college-level courses.
- Continuing - Non-Credit courses offered to the community for personal development and interest.
- Industry Training - Contracted training and education wherein a local company pays the college to provide specific training or courses for their employees.

Within the Transfer Education category, comprehensive schools typically have articulation agreements in place that provide prearranged acceptance into specific four-year institutions. At some community colleges, the partnering four-year institution teaches the third and fourth year courses at the community college location and thereby allows a student to obtain a four year degree without having to physically move to the four-year school.

There are a number of institutions and organizations which provide community college research to inform practice and policy.

COMMUNITY COLLEGE RESEARCH

There are a number of research organizations and publications who focus upon the activities of community college, junior college, and technical college institutions. Many of these institutions and organizations present the most current research and practical outcomes at annual community college conferences.

- The American Association of Community Colleges has provided oversight on community college research since the 1920s. AACC publishes a research journal called the Community College Journal.
- The mission of the Community College Research Center from Teachers College at Columbia University is to "conduct research on the major issues affecting community colleges in the United States and to contribute to the development of practice and policy that expands access to higher education and promotes success for all students."
- The Community College Survey of Student Engagement at the University of Texas at Austin is used to measure various research aspects between faculty and students in the United States.
- The Community College Futures Assembly is an annual conference to showcase the best practices in community college administration. Focus groups convene at the conference to serve as a "think tank" to inform practice of community college board of trustees, presidents, and policy makers.

Additionally, several peer-reviewed journals extensively publish research on community colleges:

- Community College Journal of Research and Practice
- New Directions for Community Colleges
- Community College Review
- The Kellogg Community College Leadership Legacy Project, researching and reporting on the success of those bringing leadership to Community Colleges and who were supported in their doctoral programs by grants by the W.K. Kellogg Foundation.
- Journal of Applied Research in the Community College

Further Education

Further education is a term mainly used in connection with education in the United Kingdom and the Republic of Ireland. It is post-compulsory education (in addition to that received at secondary school), that is distinct from the education offered in universities (higher education). It may be at any level above compulsory education, from basic training to Higher National Diploma or Foundation Degree.

A distinction is usually made between FE and higher education ("HE") which is education at a higher level than secondary school, usually provided in distinct institutions such as universities. FE in the United Kingdom therefore includes education for people over 16, usually excluding universities. It is primarily taught in FE colleges (which are similar in concept to United States community colleges, and sometimes use "community college" in their title), work-based learning, and adult and community learning institutions. This includes post-16 courses similar to those taught at schools and sub-degree courses similar to those taught at higher education (HE) colleges (which also teach degree-level courses) and at some universities.

FURTHER EDUCATION BY COUNTRY

Australia

In Australia, technical and further education or TAFE institutions provide a wide range of predominantly vocational tertiary education courses, mostly qualifying courses under the National Training System/Australian Qualifications Framework/Australian Quality Training Framework. Fields covered include hospitality, tourism, construction, engineering, secretarial skills, visual arts, information technology and community work.

Individual TAFE institutions (usually with many campuses) are known as either colleges or institutes, depending on the state or territory. TAFE colleges are owned, operated and financed by the various state and territory governments. This is in contrast to the higher education sector, whose funding is predominantly the domain of the Commonwealth government and whose universities are predominantly owned by the state governments.

UNITED KINGDOM

England

Since 2001, FE in England has been managed by the Learning and Skills Council (LSC), the largest government agency funding education provision. The LSC has a budget of some £13 billion and is organised on a regional basis through around 47 local councils. The LSC has a particular mission to improve and expand further education provision, driven by the UK government's desire to increase standards in post-16 student retention and achievement, particularly in skills-based vocational provision in FE colleges.

Recent government-driven LSC and Department for Children, Schools and Families policies, such as Success for All and the Skills Strategy, articulate this vision.The Learning and Skills Improvement Service (LSIS - formerly the Quality Improvement Agency and Centre for Excellence in Leadership)is the sector owned body supporting the development of excellent and sustainable FE provision across the learning and skills sector. Its aim is to accelerate the drive for excellence and, working in partnership with all parts of the sector, builds on the sector's own capacity to design, commission and deliver improvement and strategic change.

The Learning and Skills Network LSN offers training and consultancy.

Colleges in England that are regarded as part of the FE sector include:

- General FE and tertiary colleges
- Sixth form colleges
- Specialist colleges (mainly colleges of agriculture and horticulture and colleges of drama and dance)
- Adult education institutes

In addition, FE courses may be offered in the school sector, both in sixth form (16-19) schools, or, more commonly, sixth forms within secondary schools.

From September 2007, teachers working in FE in England are required to gain professional status, known as Qualified Teacher Learning and Skills (QTLS). The first stage of QTLS is an initial 'passport to teaching' module. The second stage is full teacher training, which would typically take up to five years to complete. The qualification covers both taught and practical skills, and also requires teachers to undertake 30 hours of continuous professional development per year.

Good quality support for employers is indicated by the award of the Training Quality Standard, an initiative to improve the quality of provision for vocational education, while all colleges and FE providers are subject to regular inspections by Ofsted.

Lifelong Learning UK is the independent sector skills council responsible for the qualifications and standards for teachers working in FE. The trade unions for FE staff are the University and College Union and the Association of Teachers and Lecturers. Teachers working in the sixth form colleges, sixth form schools and sixth forms of secondary schools are eligible to join the teaching unions which recruit in the secondary school sector

In England, further education is often seen as forming one part of a wider learning and skills sector, alongside workplace education, prison education, and other types of non-school, non-university education and training. Since June 2009, the sector is overseen by the new Department for

Business, Innovation and Skills, although some parts (such as education and training for 14-19 year olds) fall within the Department for Children, Schools and Families.

Northern Ireland

Further education in Northern Ireland is provided through six multi-campus colleges . Northern Ireland's Department for Employment and Learning has the responsibility for providing FE in the province.

- Belfast Metropolitan College
- North West Regional College
- Northern Regional College
- South Eastern Regional College
- South West College
- Southern Regional College

Most secondary schools also provide a Sixth Form scheme whereby a student can choose to attend said school for 2 additional years to complete their AS and A-levels.

Scotland

Scotland's further education colleges provide education for those young people who follow a vocational route after the end of compulsory education at age 16. They offer a wide range of vocational qualifications to young people and older adults, including SVQs, Higher National Certificates and Higher National Diplomas. Frequently, the first two years of higher education, usually in the form of an HND can be taken in an FE college, followed by attendance at university.

Wales

Further education in Wales is provided through:

- Sixth form colleges
- FE colleges

- High school sixth form within secondary schools

Further education in Wales comes under the remit of the Welsh Assembly Government and was formerly funded by ELWa before its merger with the Assembly.

Chapter–9

SCHOOLS' EDUCATIONAL TOURISM

A school is an institution designed for the teaching of students (or "pupils") under the supervision of teachers. Most countries have systems of formal education, which is commonly compulsory. In these systems, students progress through a series of schools. The names for these schools vary by country (discussed in the Regional section below), but generally include primary school for young children and secondary school for teenagers who have completed primary education. An institution where higher education is taught, is commonly called a university college or university.

In addition to these core schools, students in a given country may also attend schools before and after primary and secondary education. Kindergarten or pre-school provide some schooling to very young children (typically ages 3-5). University, vocational school, college or seminary may be available after secondary school. A school may also be dedicated to one particular field, such as a school of economics or a school of dance. Alternative schools may provide nontraditional curriculum and methods.

There are also non-government schools, called private schools. Private schools may be for children with special needs when the government does not supply for them;

religious, such as Christian schools, hawzas, yeshivas, and others; or schools that have a higher standard of education or seek to foster other personal achievements. Schools for adults include institutions of corporate training, Military education and training and business schools.

In homeschooling and online schools, teaching and learning take place outside of a traditional school building.

The schools running the Education in Switzerland include some of the most famous and oldest in the country. The main concern of the organization is the furtherance of the quality of the schools which belong to it. In Switzerland about 100,000 pupils, students and apprentices, from a wide variety of regions within our country and from over one hundred other countries, are educated in private schools.

In addition, Switzerland is proud to have some of the best private hotel schools and private universities located in the country. Summer camps, language courses and a large choice of other educational offers complete the "menu" of Swiss private education.

EF is the world leader in international education and student travel, with 45 years of experience and schools and offices in more than 50 countries. Teachers and schools choose us because we support them every step of the way as they plan their fully accredited educational tour. Students love us because a global experience forever changes lives. And parents value us because our all-inclusive trips feature guaranteed lowest prices.

Tourism management institutes in Europe are found in almost all the nations included in European Union. Some of them have gained world popularity because of their unique course pattern, highly charged study atmosphere and diversity in their outlook. These institutes offer all types of associate, certificate, diploma, graduate and undergraduate courses. A few of the best tourism management schools in Europe include:

Vatel: International Business Schools for Hotel and Tourism Management in France

Vatel in France is a widely respected hospitality and tourism management school. It is part of the world legacy of Vatel which is committed for producing students for higher as well as middle management positions in tourism sector. Tourism courses imparted by this institute generally take three to five years. Some of the most preferred courses offered by Vatel in France include Bachelor Degree in International Hotel Management and MBA in International Hospitality Management.

Les Roches: International School of Hotel Management, Switzerland

This premier tourism educational institute is included among one of the best tourism management schools in Europe. It has the legacy of producing high-profile executives and managers belonging to tourism industry. Top hospitality employers from around the world visit the campus of the institute to handpick their future managers.

Some of the most sought after hospitality courses offered by Les Roches include Swiss Hotel Association Management Diploma, MBA in Hospitality, Finance or Marketing, Bachelor of Business Administration- Hospitality (BBA) and Post-Graduate and Professional Development Studies in International Hospitality.

SHANNON COLLEGE OF HOTEL MANAGEMENT, IRELAND

This world renowned hospitality and tourism school is committed to deliver high level of educational excellence. Young aspirants prefer the school for its excellent teaching, excellent professional practice and excellent grooming qualities. This tourism school is best known for its graduate course named Bachelor of Business Studies or BBS. This four-year degree program trains the students for senior management positions in international hotel management industry.

Schiller International University, Madrid

The Madrid-based campus of this international university bears a truly cosmopolitan outlook. This prestigious hospitality and tourism school is busy in keeping up the tradition of excellence of the Spanish education. Students at this university have the choice of pursuing both graduate and undergraduate degree programs.

Graduate School Introduction

The purpose of seeking a graduate school degree varies from individual to individual, but the most common reasons for seeking a graduate degree are the following:

1. A junior or senior in college wanting to do advanced work in a subject
2. A profession that requires specialized training such as medicine, law, or social work
3. A career that has climaxed and requires advanced education to jump start it

For whichever reason you are deciding to go back to school or continue with your education, this step must be taken carefully and be well planned. Going to graduate school is a tremendous investment of time and financial resources, and you must make sure that investment will advance your career in the desired direction. Preparing yourself to make this decision is a multiple step process. First, you must look within yourself at your current pathway and your proposed destination. You will need to analyze your strength, weaknesses, financial situation, and social situation. You will also need to prioritize your needs. Then set short term and long term goals to help you keep your eye on the prize. This will require much research and footwork as well as compromising.

Attending grad school can be one of the best decisions a person can make. Not only will it help you earn more money in the long run, but odds are you'll enjoy a much higher level of job and career satisfaction while you're earning your money. In our Grad School Guide, you'll read about the benefits and challenges of attending grad school, and learn how to pick the right school for you, as well as all your different options for financing your graduate education. In our guide, you'll find lots of helpful information, much of which you've probably never really thought about before. Having all the facts can help you make a more informed decision.

Graduate Exams

In order to get into graduate school, you'll probably have to take one of these graduate exams:

- DAT Test
- GMAT Test
- GRE Test
- GRE Subject Test
- LSAT Test
- MAT Test

PLANNING YOUR SCHOOL VISIT

1. Visit The Schools

A critical part of choosing a school is actually visiting it. Your visit could be an overnight visit, an open house or a guided tour.

Many boarding schools have overnight visits. These are a terrific way of letting your child experience boarding school life. Day schools generally have open houses, and since you probably live close by, this will accomplish the same purpose. Let's face it: seeing faculty, staff and students in a variety of settings will just confirm or deny a lot of hunches you might have had in the first place. This is a most worthwhile exercise. Take advantage of it. If you have traveled any distance to see a school, you will want to have a guided tour of the facilities at the same time as your interview.

2. Plan Your Visit

If the school only gives a tour followed by an interview, then make your travel plans accordingly. School admissions offices will generally have a list of local lodgings. Ask for it. The important thing to do is to plan on getting there the night before the tour so that you and your child can both get a good night's rest. Remember: this is an exciting, stressful time for both of you.

3. Prepare Questions

Before you leave home, make sure that you have written down all the questions you have about the school. Make a list of things which you want to see. Then use your travel time and mealtimes to review this list. Don't be afraid to refer to it during the tour and the interview. Being organized and efficient will impress the admissions staff.

4. Be Prepared

The day of the tour has finally arrived! Be sure to rise early, eat a nourishing meal, and get to the school ten to fifteen minutes early. It is always smart to know where on campus you have to go and to allow time for parking and rest stops!

5. Dress To Impress

The school visit is not the appropriate time for a fashion statement from either parent or child. That would be a mistake. So dress sensibly and comfortably. Be yourself. Remember that the process works both ways: you are looking over the school, and the school is looking over you.

THE TOUR GUIDE

In most cases your tour guide will be a student. He or she will probably make written observations about you. So be alert. If you are not in a group tour, be sure to ask pertinent questions and be interested in the facts which are mentioned by the guide. Even if you have decided that you can't stand this school, good manners require that you put on your best face and soldier on.

It's a Wrap

When the tour is over, spend a few minutes reviewing your impressions and comparing notes. This information will be useful when you make your final choice.

School Tourism

Tourism is the fastest growing industry in the world, contributing 9.3% to the world economy . The UN World Tourism Organization forecasts that by 2020 over 1.56 billion international travelers will make journeys from their home countries. This unprecedented growth means there will be a need for tourism professionals to serve the industry now and in the future. The Tourism School (in time) will provide courses on aspects of tourism planning, management and sustainable development for those planning to join the industry.

A school is a large organizational structure which can contain various departments and divisions. The departments and divisions should be listed in the departments and divisions section. The school should not contain any learning resources. The school can contain projects for developing learning resources.

DIVISIONS AND DEPARTMENTS

Divisions and Departments of the School exist on pages in "topic" namespace. Start the name of departments with the "Topic:" prefix; departments reside in the Topic: namespace. Departments and divisions link to learning materials and learning projects. Divisions can link subdivisions or to departments. For more information on schools, divisions and departments look at the Naming Conventions.

Travel Planning

The concept of grouping students together in a centralized location for learning has existed since Classical antiquity. Formal schools have existed at least since ancient Greece , ancient Rome ancient India, and ancient China. The Byzantine Empire had an established schooling system beginning at the primary level. According to Traditions and Encounters, the founding of the primary education system began in 425 A.D. and "... military personnel usually had at least a primary education ...". The sometimes efficient and often large government of the Empire meant that educated citizens were a must. Although Byzantium lost much of the grandeur of Roman culture and extravagance in the process of surviving, the Empire emphasized efficiency in its war manuals. The Byzantine education system continued until the empire's collapse in 1453 AD.

Islam was another culture that developed a school system in the modern sense of the word. Emphasis was put on knowledge, which required a systematic way of teaching and spreading knowledge, and purpose-built structures. At first, mosques combined both religious performance and learning activities, but by the ninth century, the Madrassa was introduced, a proper school that was built independently from the mosque. They were also the first to make the Madrassa system a public domain under the control of the Caliph. The Nizamiyya madrasa is considered by consensus of scholars to be the earliest surviving school, built towards 1066 CE by Emir Nizam Al-Mulk.

Under the Ottomans, the towns of Bursa and Edirne became the main centers of learning. The Ottoman system of Kulliye, a building complex containing a mosque, a hospital, madrassa, and public kitchen and dining areas, revolutionized the education system, making learning accessible to a wider public through its free meals, health care and sometimes free accommodation.

The nineteenth century historian, Scott holds that a remarkable correspondence exists between the procedure established by those institutions and the methods of the present day. They had their collegiate courses, their prizes for proficiency in scholarship, their oratorical and poetical contests, their commencements and their degrees. In the department of medicine, a severe and prolonged examination, conducted by the most eminent physicians of the capital, was exacted of all candidates desirous of practicing their profession, and such as were unable to stand the test were formally pronounced incompetent.

In Europe during the Middle Ages and much of the Early Modern period, the main purpose of schools (as opposed to universities) was to teach the Latin language. This led to the term grammar school, which in the United States informally refers to a primary school, but in the United Kingdom means a school that selects entrants based on ability or aptitude. Following this, the school curriculum has gradually broadened to include literacy in the vernacular language as well as technical, artistic, scientific and practical subjects.

Chapter–10

UNIVERSITY AND COLLEGE STUDENT TOURISM

A college tour is a series of campus visits to a number of colleges or universities (two or four year) by a prospective student (freshman, transfer, or graduate.) College tours may be taken individually or by school groups and educational programs as a way for a large number of people to visit several schools over a short period of time. In addition, many colleges now offer virtual tours on the Internet.

A college tour is composed of multiple, distinct campus visits. In most cases a campus visit involves an information session directed by an admissions officer and a walking tour of campus conducted by a student ambassador. A campus visit can be taken by individual students and their families, with the student and parents often joining other individuals to create a larger group.

Many colleges offer "open houses" usually consisting of a day or series of days set aside for students and their families to visit a particular school. Often there will be special programs or presentations during these times which would not be available during a regular visit. Most colleges and universities also offer private tours and information sessions for large groups from a single school or educational program.

Counselors and admissions officers often urge students to visit colleges before applying. Students often use their observations from college visits to make a final selection.

College tours are usually planned 2 to 4 weeks in advance and more for larger schools.. Students are encouraged to plan their visit during the school year when classes are in session to get a true sense campus life. A family campus visit can be arranged by calling the school's visitor center or admissions office. Many colleges allow students to register for their college tour on the campus website. Group campus tours are planned by high school counselors, parent-teacher associations, and educational programs such as Boys and Girls Club of America or Upward Bound. Tour operators also offer paid services to plan and arrange college tours for groups in addition to transportation, lodging and activities.

Information Session

An admissions information session provides prospective students with knowledge about the college they are applying to. These sessions usually last thirty minutes to an hour and include information about admissions requirements, financial aid, and academic requirements for acceptance to that particular institution.

Campus Tour

The walking campus tour allows students to see the campus including academic buildings, residence halls, dining halls, athletic fields, and other areas. Some tours offer students a glimpse into a dorm or classroom but this varies from campus to campus. Walking tours are usually conducted by a current student ambassador who, in addition to pointing out campus highlights, answers student questions.

Tour Operator

A tour operator typically combines tour and travel components to create a holiday. The most common example of a tour operator's product would be a flight on a charter airline plus a transfer from the airport to a hotel and the services of a local representative, all for one price. Niche tour operators may specialise in destinations, e.g. Italy, activities and experiences, e.g. skiing, or a combination thereof. The original raison d'etre of tour operating was the difficulty of making arrangements in far-flung places, with problems of language, currency and communication. The advent of the internet has led to a rapid increase in self-packaging of holidays.

However, tour operators still have their competence in arranging tours for those who do not have time to do DIY holidays, and specialize in large group events and meetings such as conferences or seminars. Also, tour operators still exercise contracting power with suppliers (airlines, hotels, other land arrangements, cruises, etc.) and influence over other entities (tourism boards and other government authorities) in order to create packages and special departures for destinations otherwise difficult and expensive to visit.

The three major tour operator associations in the U.S. are the National Tour Association (NTA), the United States Tour Operators Association (USTOA), and the American Tour Association (ATA). In Europe, it is the European Tour Operators Association (ETOA), and in the UK, it is the Association of British Travel Agents (ABTA) and the Association of Independent Tour Operators (AITO). The primary association for receptive North American inbound tour operators is the Receptive Services Association of America (RSAA).

United States Tour Operators Association

The United States Tour Operators Association (USTOA) is a 501(c) registered nonprofit professional association representing the tour operator industry. Its members are made up of companies whose tours, vacation packages, and custom arrangements encompass the entire globe but who conduct business in the U.S.

As a voice for the tour operator industry, USTOA represents this sector in matters pertaining to the travel industry as a whole, both in the U.S. and abroad. Among USTOA's goals are consumer protection and education, and its high standards and work in this area have earned USTOA the endorsement of the United States Government's Consumer Action Handbook .

USTOA member companies must meet a number of ethical and financial criteria , including participation in the association's Travelers Assistance Program, which among other things protects consumer payments up to $1 million in case the company goes out of business.

Mission

USTOA's mission is focused on improving industry standards and consumer advocacy through the following:

- Inform the travel industry, government agencies and the public about tour operators' activities and objectives.
- Educate consumers on matters pertaining to tours and vacation packages.
- Help consumers recoup financial loss arising from an Active Corporate Member's bankruptcy or insolvency.
- Help maintain a high level of professionalism within the tour operator industry.
- Represent the tour operator community and cooperate with other trade organizations and government agencies.
- Facilitate and encourage tourism on a worldwide basis.

Principles

USTOA Active Corporate Members pledge to adhere to the following principles:

Ethical Conduct: Members must conduct business with competence and professionalism, representing truthfully and accurately all facts, conditions and requirements relating to their tours and travel packages.

Truth In Advertising: Advertising and quoting of prices must clearly show total deliverable prices, accurately identifying facilities, accommodations and services used. Any changes or substitutions must be communicated expeditiously to the travel agent and/or client involved.

Ethical and Financial Responsibility: Active members' business conduct must instill confidence in their financial stability, reliability and integrity.

Membership Categories and Standards

USTOA has three categories of membership: Active, Associate, and Allied.

Active Corporate Members must meet the definition of a tour operator. In addition, they must:

- have 16 references from reputable travel industry organizations, plus two from USTOA Active Members.
- be in business at least three years under same ownership and/or management.
- meet specific minimums in terms of passengers and/or sales volume.
- carry minimum $1,000,000 of professional Travel Agent/Tour Operator liability insurance, with worldwide coverage.
- participate in USTOA's Travelers Assistance Program, which among other requirements,

stipulates that each Active Corporate USTOA member post a $1 million bond to help protect consumers in case of bankruptcy or other insolvency.

Associate Members are organizations, common carriers and suppliers of tour products and services, other entities connected with travel not directly serving travelers on tour itineraries. Includes Worldwide Airlines, Car Rental Companies, Hotel/Resort/Restaurant Groups, Tourist Boards, Trade Associations.

Allied Members are carriers (other than common carriers) and suppliers whose products or services bring them into contact with travelers on tour itineraries. Includes Advertising & Public Relations, Airlines (Local), Airport Authorities, Attractions, Cruise Operators, Financial Services, Ground Tour Operators, Independent Hotels/Restaurants/Resorts, Insurance & Medical Assistance, Legal Services, Marketing & Travel Related Services, Media, Technology & Reservations Systems, Trade Shows, Visa and Passport Services.

CHAPTER–11

ISSUES

Racially motivated attacks occur in Ukraine while police and courts do little to intervene, the Council of Europe said in a report made public February 2008 in Strasbourg. The report also expressed concern about attacks against rabbis and Jewish students, as well as the vandalism of synagogues, cemeteries and cultural centres. "However, criminal legislation against racially-motivated crimes has not been strengthened and the authorities have not yet adopted a comprehensive body of civil and administrative anti-discrimination laws", the body said. "There have been very few prosecutions against people who make anti-Semitic statements or publish anti-Semitic literature." Discrimination against the Roma community, continuing anti-Semitism, violence in Crimea and other acts of intolerance against various ethnic groups in Ukraine were singled out in the report by the Council of Europe's racism-monitoring body, the European Commission against Racism and Intolerance.

Skinhead violence against Tatars and Jews is also frequent and police have offered little protection to the different communities, it said. And ECRI asked Ukrainian authorities to step up efforts to fight violence by skinheads against Africans, Asians, and people from the Middle East For instance: in December 2006 racist attacks on foreign students have been reported by the Council of Europe.

The council stated that students where reluctant to report attacks because of police response to these attacks seemed to be inadequate. Many of these incidents are conducted by "skinheads" or neo-Nazis in Kiev, but similar crimes have also been reported throughout the country. In addition to incidents of assault, persons of African or Asian heritage may be subject to various types of harassment, such as being stopped on the street by both civilians and law enforcement officials. Individuals belonging to religious minorities have also been harassed and assaulted in Kiev and throughout Ukraine

Ukraine does not currently have well established movements against illegal immigration or certain ethnic groups that are common in other former Soviet states. As a European country Ukraine is prone to outside influence from the neo-nazi and supremacist movements beyond its borders. For example, in areas of Southern Ukraine that have closer cultural and linguistic ties with Russia a number of neo-nazi groups resemble those in neighbouring Russia.

Since 2005, nongovernmental (NGO) monitors in Ukraine have documented a dramatic rise in violent crimes with a suspected bias motivation. While incidents occurring in Kiev have been most accurately documented, there is evidence that incidents of violence are taking place throughout the country, including the cities of Cherkasy, Chernivtsi, Kharkiv, Luhansk, Lutsk, Lviv, Mykolaiv, Odessa, Sevastopol, Simferopol, Ternopil, Vinnytsia, and Zhytomyr.

Representatives of the Ministry of Justice and Members of Ukrainian parliament stated that discrimination views and antisocial attitudes are practiced by a minority of the population, by fringe organizations, and by younger generation of Ukrainians; they say they are most alarmed by the younger Ukrainian's attitudes. The fact that, during the 2007 parliamentary elections, the right wing parties espousing xenophobic and racist ideology received very little support from the electorate, also points to the unpopularity of such ideas among the general population.

Bias-motivated violence has been largely committed against people of African and Asian origin, as well as people from the Middle East.

New Discoveries- new knowledge, New Insights- are never homogeneous. Diversity allows for new shapes, textures and imaginings of knowledge; it encourages the innovation and insight that is essential to the creation of knowledge. A diverse community of scholars asks diverse questions and has diverse insights, and so pushes the forefront of knowledge further, faster.

Diversity create a more dynamic intellectual environment and a richer educational experience. A diverse environment fosters a plurality of perspectives. It creates the possibility of discourse and learning by talented people of various cultures, backgrounds and experiences.

DIVERSITY IN U.S. UNIVERSITIES

Supporting diversity and creating a sense of inclusiveness for minority and international students are growing priorities for U.S. graduate schools. The University of Virginia has recently been awarded for its new program to support graduate student diversity . The graduate study at U.S university offers opportunity for students to come together, challenge each others ideas, learn new perspectives and grow as individuals. It holds out the hope that the next generation of leaders will understand that our differences are our strengths, that our diversity can be the essence of our excellence. Diverse environment at these universities helps students from all races and backgrounds to work effectively in a decidedly more diverse work place.

United States Anti-Racism Act/Laws

Considering the enormous consequences of discriminatory acts toward children in school, the United states had made various promises under the CERD, the CAT, the ICCPR, and the Programme of Action from the World Conference on Racism to eliminate the racially discriminatory practices in the American public education system.

The CERD requires every child to have a right to an education.

The ICCPR states that children have a right to be protected, irrespective of their skin color.

The CAT requires all forms of torture to be eliminated; this includes the severe mental suffering that is associated with discrimination.

The universities in U.S and Canada value the diverse community and aims to ensure that no one in the university community is disadvantaged on the grounds of race, cultural background, ethnic or national origin or religious belief. In order to combat the racial discrimination, universities like Lancaster, Kingston, Stanford etc. have adopted equal opportunities statement. The Race Relations Act ensures that issues of race equality are taken account of in all policy making, service delivery, regulation and enforcement and employment practice.

What do the Students Have to Say?

"Coming to Wilson with the opportunity to read for my bachelor's degree in international relations was the beginning of a stream of opportunities. Wilson has not only displayed all the proverbial 'windows' as options, but has also given me the opportunity to open the ones most suited to my academic interests and to gaze beyond the present. Wilson supported my Study Abroad in Beijing China as well as in London." says Jing Luan, a student at Wilson College.

"I recommend Wilson because of the variety of programs it offers its international students. One experience that I really enjoyed and learned a lot from is the NMUN (National Model United Nation) program. For this, I went to Washington D.C. and New York, and I had a chance to explore what it is like to be a diplomat. After this, I became more certain in my major and my choices for the future." says Mariam Khalifeh, a student at Wilson College.

Youth Gangs have flourished throughout many of the large cities of Australia, especially Melbourne and Sydney. There are many suburban gangs throughout Melbourne involving clashes between North-West and South-East as well as ongoing battles in Melbourne's Western Suburbs. There are many other gangs evolving throughout the outer suburbs of Brisbane as well. There have also been a few cases of Australian gangs imitating American street gangs such as the Bloods with no affiliation to the original gangs. In most cases these minor gangs are formed by bored youth influenced by the American Hip Hop scene. The internet has become a focal point for these gangs, posting pictures, post codes and sometimes even running a gang's personal website. Australian youth gangs grow in accordance to general population growth.

During the early 1990s, Melbourne youth gangs included: 3174, based around Noble Park and Springvale; Keyzy/ Burra boys, based in Keysborough; LSC, based in St. Albans through to Taylors Lakes; 14K, based in Footscray; MC3, based in Dandenong South; Oakleigh Wogs, based in Oakleigh; Springy Nips, based in Springvale.

Current gangs in Melbourne include the Richmond based Yellow Klique, city based Central Crew, the western suburbs Brothers 4 Life and Young St Albans and Kings Park, and the Springvale based Young Springy Boys. Members from Yellow Klique and Central Crew had formed alliances and are currently at war with Brothers 4 Life. This gang war has seen an increase in knife attacks amongst young Asian men as well as a rise in bottle and glass related assaults. These three gangs have shown to be extremely violent even in front of police and security. Their activity has gone from assaulting one another in the streets to fire bombing of rival's houses. In 2010, a Victoria Police task force headed by Acting Detective Inspector Dave de Francesco, named Task Force Echo, was formed to counter warring gangs.

In May and June 2009, Indian media reported what it saw to be racially motivated crimes against Indians , especially students. Rallies were organised in Melbourne and Sydney, and intense coverage of the perceived hate crimes commenced in India, being especially critical of Australia and Australian police services. The Australian government initially called for calm as it investigated these crimes. In June 2009, the Victorian Chief Commissioner, Simon Overland, opined that some of the crimes were racist in nature, and others were opportunistic.

Reaction from the Australian population was generally sympathetic to the plight of the students.

Background

Indian students comprise the second largest group of international students in tertiary education in Australia. From 2004 to 2009 the number of Indians studying in Australia rose from 30,000 to 97,000 with 45,000 of these living in Melbourne, 32,000 in Adelaide and the remainder shared between Sydney, Brisbane and Perth. Some come from the rural parts of India, with most coming to Australia to seek permanent residency. Eapen Verghese argued in an opinion piece that the cost of living in Australian cities has made it necessary for many of these students to live in cheaper and more distant suburbs, where there is an increased risk of encountering violent crime. Others have argued that Indian student face discrimination and exploitation in housing and jobs.

In 2007-2008, international education contributed A$13.7 billion to the Australian economy, measured through all categories of export earnings, including tuition fees, living expenses and tourism associated with visits from relatives. Inder Panjwani, General Secretary of the Association of Australian Education Representatives in India (AAERI) stated there was a possibility that a few Indian students who had been admitted to Australian universities might cancel their admissions [because they feared attacks].

Chronology

2007-2008 Assaults

In the year 2007-2008, 1,447 Indians were victims of crime including assaults and robberies in the state of Victoria in Australia. However, the statistics reportedly show that Indians were not over represented in assaults. In either case, the Victorian police refused to release the data for public scrutiny, the stated reason being that it was "problematic: as well as 'subjective and open to interpretation'".

April 2008 Indian Taxi Driver Protest

On 29 April 2008, in Melbourne an estimated five hundred Indian taxi drivers protested at Flinders Street Station with a sit-in protest following the death of a taxi driver. A similar protest was held on 19 May 2008 in Adelaide, where about fifty taxi drivers protested after an assault on an Indian taxi driver. The Victorian Government brought in mandatory safety shields later that year, but this was met with protests because of the costs.

May 2009 Indian Student Protests

After incidents in May 2009, over 4,000 Indian Students staged a protest opposite Federation Square in Melbourne on 31 May 2009, saying the attacks were motivated out of racism and were not being sufficiently addressed by the Australian Government. One report said "Along with more police protection, the students also want a multicultural police section, and on-site accommodation for Indian students at all universities and colleges". 18 protesters were arrested.

On 31 May 2009, In Melbourne India's High Commissioner, Sujatha Singh, met with Victorian State Premier John Brumby to express her government's concerns over the violence. On 1 June 2009, Indian Prime Minister Manmohan Singh phoned Prime Minister Kevin Rudd to express his concerns.

On 1 June 2009, in New Delhi about a 100 people including members of the Indian far-right Shiv Sena and student protesters held a demonstration outside the Australian High Commission in New Delhi, where effigies of Kevin Rudd were burnt. Shiv Sena MP Manohar Joshi warned that Australians living or travelling in India could face revenge attacks if Indians living in Australia continued to be attacked. On the same day Australian Prime Minister Kevin Rudd expressed regret for the attacks and declared that the perpetrators would be brought to justice. He did not state whether he considers the attacks to be racially motivated.

The left-wing All India Students Federation conducted a candle march at the India Gate, and demanded "stringent action against those behind the brutal attacks on the innocent students".

In June 2009, Indian student organisations called on the Indian government to declare Australia an "unsafe destination for Indian students"., the National Students Union of India met the Minister of State of External Affairs, Shashi Tharoor and demanded that the Centre should prevail upon the Australian government to ensure that such incidents do not occur again and the Vishwa Hindu Parishad political party, said it would consider an Australian boycott over the bashings if authorities did not do more to protect Hindus in Australia.

On 7 to 10 June 2009, rallies in the Sydney CBD and at Harris Park, were attended by hundreds of Indians and supporters. The rally started at Sydney Town Hall and marched to Hyde Park. Some attending the rally specifically mentioned Harris Park (a Sydney suburb where 20% of the population is Indian), as an area where Indians were frequently assaulted, and called on police to do more to make that suburb safe. The students said they were considered "soft targets". Some Indian protestors were reported to be carrying hockey sticks and baseball bats. According to police, the protest was sparked by an attack on Indians earlier in the evening allegedly by Lebanese men. In retaliation the protesters attacked three uninvolved Lebanese men, who sustained minor injuries. This was believed to be the first violent reaction by Indian students against attacks on them. A police dog squad was called in to control the crowd.

On 9 June 2009, Indian Prime Minister, addressing the Indian Parliament said that "he was 'appalled' by the senseless violence and crime, some of which are racist in nature,"

On 4 July 2009 Michael Danby heading a six-member Australian parliamentarian delegation to India said, "We are joining the Premier of Victoria in a march to express the views of the overwhelming majority of Australians condemning these attacks.", but when the Harmony Day March Occurred On 12 July 2009 , FISA was not given leave to address the crowd.

In September 2009, Victorian Premier John Brumby visited India at the end of September and tried to "repair Australia's reputation" as fewer Indian students are applying for Australian visas.

January 2010 Protests

Two murders on 29 December 2009 and 3 January 2010 resulted in a protest in New Delhi.

On 5 January 2010, A cartoon depicting the Victoria Police as a Ku Klux Klan member was published in the New Delhi Mail Today This was condemned by Acting Prime Minister Julia Gillard who described it as "deeply offensive". In January 2010 the Indian Government issued a travel advisory for Indians in Melbourne, warning of the increasing crime rate "often accompanied by verbal abuse and fueled by drugs and alcohol". However, Simon Crean, the acting Foreign Minister, urged Indian leaders to "avoid fuelling hysteria" and stated that Melbourne was a safe place to visit.

On 26 January 2010, the Prime Minister's nephew Van Thanh Rudd and Sam King, dressed up as members of the Ku Klux Klan, protesting against the racist violence against Indians in Melbourne, with the signs "Racism - Made in Australia" on the front of their dresses. The protest took place in front of Melbourne Park and both were arrested within 10 minutes.

On 24 February 2010, the Vindaloo against Violence protest saw 17,000 protesters at over 400 restaurants, workplaces, schools and universities "reached out to the Indian community, and all our immigrant communities, to let them know that they are not indifferent to violence and that they are welcome and entitled to feel safe here. showed the government and law enforcement that we feel seriously about this issue and want to understand why this violence is happening and what is being done to diffuse it. The official participation of Victoria Police and Premier Brumby in the day's action illustrates that this message has been received."

November 2010 Stabbing

Another student was stabbed in the stomach on 5 November 2010 in Melbourne. Police reported that they believed the attack to have been random, rather than racially motivated.

Reactions

Media Coverage

Indian community leaders in Australia said Indian media has blown the issue out of proportion, and that their coverage could overcast the real issues faced by students.

The Indian media's coverage has been likened to hysteria by the Australian media. Australia's Immigration Minister, Chris Evans, said "There's been a lot of concern inside India and there's been, I think, some fairly hysterical reporting of what's occurred." The Herald Sun's conservative right wing columnist, Andrew Bolt, described the events as a "circus", whilst another said that Indian TV networks ignored the higher murder rate in India. The Victorian Premier said the Indian media's coverage of the incidents was "unbalanced" and emphasised that two Indian nationals were charged with the murder of Jaspreet Singh.

On 8 Feb 2010, the weekly Indian newsmagazine Outlook published a 10-page cover story on the attacks called "Why the Aussies Hate Us", in which Vinod Mehta, the editor in chief wrote that the Indian Media were not overreacting in their coverage of the violence, and accused the Australian authorities of displaying a "smug and superior attitude". He expressed admiration for Australia but criticized the Australian responses.

Some in the Indian media have accused the Australian authorities of being denialist.

There were also concerns that reports of an Indian journalist being attacked in Australia, cited by several Indian newspapers as an example of the "ongoing attacks," did not mention that her assailant was Indian.

In an attempt to repair the relationship, some Indian journalists were invited to visit Australia.

Racism

A report about attacks on Indians in Australia was submitted to the Indian Parliament by the Overseas Indian Ministry, early 2010. According to this report, of the 152 attacks that the Indian consulate was aware of, 23 had "racial overtones", i.e., were accompanied by racial abuse, or "anti-Indian remarks". The majority were found to be either thefts, or robberies, or results of verbal disputes.

Yadu Singh, a cardiologist who heads the Indian Student Welfare Committee set up by the Indian Consulate in Sydney, said there had been at least 20 beatings of Indian students in Sydney in the past month, but most went unreported out of fear. He estimated over 100 attacks on Indian students in the last 12 months. He described the phenomenon as "curry bashing", and that "They are not random at all, the people are targeting them. They know these students are easy targets." He labelled the Indian press' reporting of the incidents as "irresponsible". Dr Singh believed Australians were "outraged with the way Indian media" was smearing the country. He went on to say that other Indians he had spoken to said they are not suffering and that they are doing well in Australia. He also expressed fear that the Indian media reports might lead to backlash against other Indian Australians. Others have objected to labeling Australia as racist based on the actions of a few.

Sitaram Yechury, a member of parliament representing the Communist Party of India (Marxist), wrote that both sides of the debate have points. Economic crises and downfalls often cause rising fascism and racism against minorities, such as the rise of Nazi Germany, the Great American Depression, as well as economic downturns in India itself resulting in racist-like violence between various ethnic groups and ultra-nationalist parties in the country. Yechury says that the racism directed against Indians in Australia can be explained in this broader context.

Chief Executive of Primus Telecommunications Australia, Ravi Bhatia, said the Australian government has shown "excellent sensitivity" towards the issue by announcing a slew of measures like Harmony march, reforms in the state sentencing law and setting up of Task Force to deal with attacks on Indian students. On 5 January 2010, A cartoon depicting the Victoria Police as a Ku Klux Klan member was published in the New Delhi Mail Today This was condemned by Acting Prime Minister Julia Gillard who described it as "deeply offensive".

Nama Nageswara Rao, leader of the Telugu Desam Party, visited Australia, and held a press conference on his return. He stated that he had interviewed many of the victims, and the attacks did not appear to be motivated by racism. He also noted that many of the perpetrators were immigrants from ethnic minorities, such as "Afghans, Lebanese and other nationals who settled in Australia". Sydney students interviewed by ABC's AM programme stated that their attackers were from a range of ethnic backgrounds, and while they said there was a "racial element" they also saw the attacks as opportunistic. The attackers have been described as being white, African, Asian, Middle Eastern, Aboriginal, and Pacific Islander.

Herald Sun columnist Andrew Bolt criticised the automatic labelling of Australia as a racist country as unfair, noting comments from foreign victims of crime that their attackers were foreigners themselves. On 28 January 2010 two Indian nationals were arrested for the murder of an Indian national killed on 29 December 2009. People from a range of different ethnic backgrounds perpetrated these assaults and investigations revealed that at least two of the later attacks were perpetrated by Indians.

Statistics Controversy

An Australian study into the statistics of these attacks concludes that "In the light of poor criminological evidence and a plethora of evocative images, the global media has propagated and fostered claims about crimes and racism related to that are well outside the evidence.".

A report was submitted to the Indian Parliament by the Overseas Indian Ministry, early 2010. According to this report, of the 152 attacks that the Indian consulate was aware of, 23 had "racial overtones", i.e., were accompanied by racial abuse, or "anti-Indian remarks". The majority were found to be either thefts, or robberies, or results of verbal disputes.

The NSW Bureau of Crime Statistics and Research states there has been no recorded increase in assault crimes in Harris Park in the past two years. A member of the NSW upper house, Gordon Moyes, cited changing victim demographics for the suburb, "What has happened over the last few years is that a number of Indian students, attracted by fairly cheap accommodation, have come into the area, the target - always the soft targets - moved from elderly people walking on the street to Indian students with laptops.

New South Wales Police have stated that Indians are not over represented in Australian crime statistics.

This view was supported by Sydney-based United India Association president Dr Prabhat Sinha, who took the view that the attacks were not necessarily racially motivated. He said: "They become soft targets by groups of four to six drug users, for example, who just want cash."

The Victorian State Premier, John Brumby, has stated that internal police statistics show that Indians are not over represented in assaults. However, according to the Police Commissioner, Simon Overland, people belonging to a broad statistical category of "South Asian appearance" (which includes Indians) are over represented in robberies. In either case, the Victorian police refuse to release these statistics to public scrutiny, the stated reason being that they are "problematic: as well as 'subjective and open to interpretation'".

Newspaper columnist Greg Sheridan said that Victorian Premier John Brumby was in "indolent denialism" regarding these incidents by saying that "Assaults on Indian students are under-represented as a population share." According to Sheridan, the Victorian Police had initially denied gathering statistics on crime by ethnicity, then reversed that and said they did collate such statistics, but said that they were unreliable. Sheridan was concerned that there was also systematic under-reporting of all crime in Victoria as claimed in the Victorian Ombudsman report "Crime Statistics and Police Numbers".

Educational, Policing and Safety Issues

Ruchir Punjabi, an Indian International student in Australia, claimed early in the debate about the cause of the events in the Sydney Morning Herald that labeling the crimes as racism was distracting from critical issues in the education sector that the Government needed to give due attention to.

An editorial in the Geelong Advertiser suggested that education institutions should take more consideration of safeguarding student safety, and other factors including inadequate policing numbers and liquor licensing should be addressed.

The Ministerial Council on Education, Employment, Training and Youth Affairs said it would conduct a national quality crackdown on education and training providers, in particular smaller education providers that have been the target of student complaints.

South Australia is the only state that has an agency responsible for international student safety. Education Adelaide, jointly funded by the state government and Adelaide City council, provides a function in the Adelaide

Town Hall hosted by the Lord Mayor to welcome new arrivals, organises social events for international students, provides them with a written guide on personal safety and safe shopping, campaigns for affordable accommodation in the city centre and provides a farewell party in Government House hosted by the Governor at the end of their stay. Following the recent media attention regarding attacks on Indian students, the agency accepted testimonials on the safety of living in Adelaide from international students, including one from the 22 year old Sikh who had been attacked in Rundle Mall on 11 June.

The People's Republic of China has also expressed concern over student safety in Australia. According to official figures, more than 130,000 Chinese students are currently studying in Australia.

New Zealand has responded to these attacks and subsequent incidents. The education sector in New Zealand has moved to distance itself from attacks on Indian students, saying they were "totally different societies". The Chief Executive of the New Zealand Education Trust, Robert Stevens, has stressed to prospective students from India that New Zealand "is a different country from Australia - in the nicest possible way", and is striving to market New Zealand to Indians in this manner. Education authorities in New Zealand are hoping recent attacks on Indian students in Australia will make New Zealand a more attractive option.

Need for a mechanism to prevent attacks on Indians abroad. Domestically, the Indian government declared that it would formulate a policy to deal with racial discrimination against Indians abroad.

As part of the initiative to create an institutionalised mechanism to prevent racist attacks on Indians abroad, Vayalar Ravi, the head of the overseas Indian affairs ministry, has been tasked to protect the Indians in Australia. Ravi has called for a report on these incidents from the Indian High Commission in Australia.

Aftermath

There was a 46% drop in Indians applying for student visas for Australia from July to 31 Oct 2009 compared to the same period in 2008, and a total drop of 26% in student visa applications to Australia from all countries (including India). A study (completed before the deaths of Nitin Garg and Ranjodh Singh) forecast a 20% drop in Indian students expected to study in Australia in 2010, compared to 2009, partly due to a reduction in the number of visas allowed to be granted, stiffening of the regulations associated with them, the strength of the Australian dollar, and a clampdown on unscrupulous migration agents and colleges. After the attacks of 2009 and the deaths in Jan 2010, its expected to fall even further than the 20% drop.

In response, Victorian police were given new powers to conduct stop-and-search operations without the need for warrants. They conducted their first stop-and-search operation for 3 hours at Footscray train station which has a history of knife crime. They found seven people carrying twelve weapons.

The former head of its elite Special Air Service (SAS) regiment and current National Security Adviser, Duncan Lewis, was charged with leading a taskforce to examine the attacks on Indian students. Lewis chaired the task force's first meeting and coordinated Australia's response to the assaults. The Victorian government is considering enacting hate crime legislation that would consider prejudicial motivation as a factor in sentencing.

In Nov 2009, Victoria's Opposition Leader, Ted Baillieu said he will permanently put 2 guards armed with guns, on every train station in Melbourne from 6pm till last train every night, if he wins the 2010 state election.

Bollywood Reaction

Bollywood's largest labour union declared that its members would refuse to work in Australia until attacks on Indian students there are stopped. Dinesh Chaturvedi, the general secretary of the Federation of Western India Cine Employees Association, has declared that their associates have been instructed not to shoot films in Australia as "the situation is not normal over there".

In response to the issue, Bollywood star Amitabh Bachchan turned down an honorary doctorate from the Queensland University of Technology. Fellow Indian actor, Aamir Khan, has condemned the attacks, stating that, "Most disturbing to hear about racist attacks on Indians living in Australia. Quite a shame. While this doesn't mean that all Australians are racists, the frequency and seriousness of such attacks, I think, calls for an extra ordinary reaction from the Australian authorities, and while we want action to be taken by authorities in Australia, equally we should remember all the various crimes against foreigners who visit India."

Students leaving

Federation of Indian Students in Australia (FISA) says that 30,000 Indian students have left Australia in the last year, and claims "race attacks is one of the major reasons behind the exodus".'Other significant factors include that there are no jobs and students can't survive without that. Denying permanent residency to many Indians despite fulfilment of conditions has also been a reason.

Chapter–12

FUTURE OF EDUCATIONAL TOURISM

Bali as educational tourism destination has to follow the goal of education program of government of Republic of Indonesia. At the local level, the local government tourism authorities, universities/colleges and tourism stakeholders will be participate in the process of identifying the appropriate themes to form the framework of educational tourism strategy.

In addition, inputs also come from travel agents or tour operator to shape the theme and product package. The implementation of the educational tourism in Bali will be based on the existing frameworks of institutions. They provide Bali a more co-coordinated approach to negotiations and strengthen their bargaining position in international market.

Creating a neighbor countries market is important because in 2008 almost 67.64 % of tourist flows to Bali resulted from Asia Pacific region where Australia is 15.68% and Japan 18.2% (Bali Government Tourism Office, 2009). Increasing number of foreign tourists visiting Bali should prepare for this new demand. The theme, curriculum, course content and schedule will be the outcome of joint efforts by all stakeholders. To facilitate the delivery of the educational tourism program, tourism stakeholders can take advantage of the University of Udayana as the oldest government university in Bali.

All jobs are fiercely contested these days - and the leisure, travel and tourism industries are no exception to that rule. In fact they are probably the strongest example of the rule as it applies to non 9 to 5 type employment. That is because leisure, travel and tourism are industries that tend to reward people who want to work and sell holiday packages full of fun and adventure. And a lot of people find that they are happier when they sell something they would like to buy themselves. That means heavy competition - and that means doing tourism studies or tourism management courses, in order to improve your chances of obtaining one of the jobs you really want to do.

The first thing to do here, of course, is to decide what you really want to do. The travel, leisure and tourism industries cover a very wide range of posts and opportunities - from flight crew or airport staff (with all the amazing perks that entails) to working in hotels or as travel agents. The point of the courses is to give you a leg up into the travel, leisure or tourism career you want to have. And that means that you first have to select the area of your interest.

That said, mind, both tourism studies and tourism management courses have an element in them of helping you decide "on the course". By taking a course in travel management or in tourist studies, you are able to actively test the waters you are about to dive into, without having to go so far as to actually take a job. So, if you think you want a career in some branch of leisure, travel or tourism, but you do not know for sure, then taking on a course module is a great way to find out. It works both ways too - if you do that, then any company that would otherwise be unsure whether or not to employ you, can judge you by looking at your results.

In a way, travel and tourism studies and tourism management courses offer an ideal alternative to the rather false environment of an interview. Your willingness to work and the way in which you work, is giving a practical airing, so your potential employer can see who you really are and how you work without having to rely solely on an interview to give them an idea.

That means that candidates who find interviews very hard can go into them knowing that they have already done a lot of the hard work. Travel and tourism studies and tourism management courses are like doing course work as well as exams - you get a huge part of your mark guaranteed and out of the way before you need to go into a test. That means you have more chance of succeeding, you are more confident and so can express yourself better.

In comparison to the earlier times, the present world brings a more sprawling educational arena suffused with academic and career-oriented courses. For all human beings, education is must and this long journey commences with a particular course. Although there are ample academic courses, a tourism degree course is worth enrolling. In fact, most of the tourism degree courses are fetching excellent opportunities. Right from undergraduates to postgraduates, diverse learning programs on tourism are also being offered. There are regular as well as distance learning tourism courses, and a successful completion of any of them can help you become travel and tourist professionals or tourist agents

Concerning the projects, external events respectively the project sometimes rise up as a surprise to the project manager and his team. It is essential for the project team to recognize that they must also be responsive to it. It includes the established and latest state-of-the-art technology in which the project is based on, its customers and competitors, its geographical, climatic, social, economic and political settings, in fact, virtually everything that can impact its success. These factors can affect the planning, organizing, staffing and directing which constitute the project manager's main responsibilities.

Bali which is located in Indonesia is the tourist destination that exist and well known in the world. Bali was named the best island in Asia Pacific and the best spa destination in the world 2009 (DestinAsian and SENSES Magazine, 2009). The number of international tourists arrived in Bali 2008 were 1,968,892 people (Bali Government Tourism Office, 2009). Bali is good destination for learning, leisure and traveling. The attractive of Bali as educational tourism for international students because of three main factors: Bali as international tourist destination, high supported infrastructure, and value for money compare to other countries. Bali educational tourism is an alternative strategy to the mass tourism developed in Bali.

There is also a need of high standard quality of human resource especially in Asia Pacific as this region is growth in industrialization and tourism development. To fulfill this requirement the high and international quality of education and international experience needed. The programs enhance the international understanding between young age's generations that will create the positive image in the future. International education tourism program also help the students to understand the home country and its position in the global context.

Internationally, educational tourism has been recognized as an important market segment in the tourism industry. Although definitions of educational tourism abounds, the best way to conceptualize the market segment is to look at the broad range of activities. These include the classic education-like school trip and study tours (referred to as a model for benign tourism by some scholars, vacation and exchange programs, under and postgraduate study programs, short courses, and language courses. Expatriates working at overseas universities are also known to arrange compulsory fieldtrips for students during their holidays.

• Noddings, Nel (1995), Philosophy of Education, Boulder, CO: Westview Press, p. 1, ISBN 0-8133-8429-X

• Pancevski, Bojan (18 April 2010). "Get packing: Brussels decrees holidays are a human right". The Sunday Times. http://www.timesonline.co.uk/tol/news/world/europe/article7100943.ece.

• Pashler, Harold; McDonald, Mark; Rohrer, Doug; Bjork, Robert (2009), "Learning Styles: Concepts and Evidence", Psychological Science in the Public Interest 9 (3): 105–119

• Potashnik, M. and Capper, J.. "Distance Education:Growth and Diversity" (PDF).

• Quinion, Michael (26 November 2005). "Dark Tourism". World Wide Words. http://www.worldwidewords.org/turnsofphrase/tp-dar2.htm. Retrieved 9 April 2010.

• Robinson, K.: Schools Kill Creativity. TED Talks, 2006, Monterrey, CA, USA.

• Samuel Bowles and Herbert Gintis, Schooling in Capitalist America: Educational Reform and the Contradictions of Economic Life (Basic Books, 1976)

• Spode, Hasso (1998). "Geschichte der Tourismuswissenschaft". In Haedrich, Günther (in German). Tourismus-management: Tourismus-marketing Und Fremdenverkehrsplanung. Berlin: [u.a.] de Gruyter. ISBN 3110151855. OCLC 243881885.

• Swassing, R. H., Barbe, W. B., & Milone, M. N. (1979). The Swassing-Barbe Modality Index: Zaner-Bloser Modality Kit. Columbus, OH: Zaner-Bloser.

• Taghioff, Daniel. "Seeds of Consensus—The Potential Role for Information and Communication Technologies in Development.". Archived from the original on 2003-10-12.

• Thomas Armstrong's website detailing Multiple Intelligences

• Tremblay, Eric. "(2010) Educating the Mobile Generation – using personal cell phones as audience response systems in post-secondary science teaching. Journal of Computers in Mathematics and Science Teaching, 29(2), 217-227. Chesapeake, VA: AACE.".

• UNESCO, Education For All Monitoring Report 2008, Net Enrollment Rate in primary education

• Whyte, Cassandra Bolyard (1989) Student Affairs-The Future.Journal of College Student Development, v30 n1 p86-89.

• Wurzburger, Rebecca; et al (2009). Creative Tourism: A Global Conversation: How to Provide Unique Creative Experiences for Travelers Worldwide: As Presented at the 2008 Santa Fe & UNESCO International Conference on Creative Tourism in Santa Fe, New Mexico, USA. Santa Fe: Sunstone Press. ISBN 9780865347243. OCLC 370387178.

INDEX